EXPLORING KARMA & REBIRTH

Nagapriya

EXPLORING
KARMA & REBIRTH

WINDHORSE PUBLICATIONS

Published everywhere except Australia and New Zealand by
Windhorse Publications
11 Park Road
Birmingham
B13 8AB, UK
email: info@windhorsepublications.com
web: www.windhorsepublications.com

Published in Australia and New Zealand by
Windhorse Books
PO Box 574
Newtown NSW 2042
Australia
email: books@www.windhorse.com.au
web: www.windhorse.com.au

Cover design by Marlene Eltschig

Printed in India by Gopsons Papers Ltd., Noida

British Library Cataloguing in Publication Data:
A catalogue record for this book is available from the British Library

ISBN-10   1 899579 61 3
ISBN-13   978 1 899579 61 7

CONTENTS

To Dharmachari Subhuti, my mentor and friend,
with thanks for all your support and guidance.

*Experiences are preceded by mind, led by mind,
and produced by mind. If one speaks or acts
with an impure mind, suffering follows
even as the cart-wheel follows the hoof
of the ox (drawing the cart).*

*Experiences are preceded by mind, led by mind,
and produced by mind. If one speaks or acts
with a pure mind, happiness follows like a shadow
that never departs.*

The Dhammapada[1]

Acknowledgements

Like all things, this book has arisen in dependence on many conditions. It began as a lecture I delivered to a conference for sixth-form students organized by the Clear Vision Trust. I would like to thank Clear Vision for stimulating me to think about these issues. I would like to thank the Dharmavastu Centre for Buddhist Inquiry for allowing me to use its library and to work on this book between teaching commitments.

I also wish to thank all those who have discussed, argued, and wondered about these issues with me. I would especially like to thank a group of students who studied Karma and rebirth with me for a week in 2001. For support, comments, and suggestions I would like to thank Dharmacharis Abhaya, Jnanaketu, Ratnaguna, Ratnaprabha, and Vadanya; and Dharmacharini Shuddhabha, Will Buckingham, Dr Steve Pettifer of the University of Manchester, and Dr Simon O'Sullivan of Goldsmiths' College, London. Finally, I would like to thank Windhorse Publications for editorial input and for getting this into print.

About the Author

Nagapriya was born in 1969, and brought up in rural South Gloucestershire. He studied philosophy at Leeds University, and came into contact with Buddhism at the Leeds Buddhist Centre. After completing his degree he moved to Manchester to pursue ordination within the Western Buddhist Order. Following his ordination in 1992, he worked as a teacher and administrator at the Manchester Buddhist Centre until 1997.

After a period of travelling, Nagapriya worked at the Dharmavastu Centre for Buddhist Inquiry from 1998 to 2003. During that time, he taught on many residential retreats, established correspondence-based Buddhist study programmes, and set up a scholarship to enable Indian Buddhists to study at Dharmavastu.

He now lives in the Manchester area and is studying for an MA in religion. He also works with dyslexic students as a study skills tutor. He has written articles for the *Western Buddhist Review*, and this is his first book.

Nagapriya's interests include the cross-cultural study of European and Asian thought, Japanese Pure Land Buddhism, and spiritual experience and Postmodernity. He is also learning Spanish.

Author's Note

Karma is a complex term with several layers of use and meaning. In contemporary English it is most commonly understood to denote something like fate or destiny. From a Buddhist point of view, such a rendering is not only inaccurate but misleading. In this book, *Karma* with a capital K signifies a general principle relating to the realm of human conduct. When rendered in lower case, it is used to mean a willed action (a *karma*) and to indicate the influence or potential of an individual's previous conduct, for example 'Nagapriya's karma'. To reach a fuller understanding of the nuances of the term, the reader will need to consult the book.

I have generally used the Sanskrit *karma* in preference to the Pali *kamma* because this has become familiar in English. Sometimes, however, such as when quoting from Pali sources, I have retained the Pali spelling.

INTRODUCTION

I was just 18 when I first came across Buddhism, but I was already wondering if my life was coming to an end. I felt lonely, deeply confused, and was verging on mental illness. I hated myself, my life, and had all but lost hope. I could see no way forward. My suffering was compounded by the view that I would always be as I was: I would always have the same habits, fears, doubts, and difficulties. I felt trapped in my own mind and was spiralling downwards into ever bleaker places. What a be-draggled, pitiable figure I must have seemed when I first appeared at the door of the tiny Leeds Buddhist Centre in 1989.

Perhaps the most liberating message that got through to me in those early difficult months of engagement with Buddhist teachings was this: I can change. This was a shaft of light that illuminated the gloom and, while it probably seems a rather obvious and even trivial insight to many, it was to me a revela-tion. For the first time, or so it seemed, I discovered that I was not fixed; I need not always be as I had been, I could become some-thing else, I could change. This discovery that I could change was a lifebelt and I clung on tightly. Since that time I have come close to slipping beneath the icy waters of oblivion more than once, but in so far as I can remember that simple insight – I can change – I can see some way forward. It was probably this teaching more than any other that convinced me that Buddhism lit up a path that I wanted to follow.

So is this conviction that we can all change the essence of Buddhism? Well, as a spiritual tradition that has evolved through more than two millennia and spread to many cultures, Buddhism is a lot more complicated than this. After hearing that initial revelatory message that I can change, I then heard many other things. I heard, for example, that I could change because I don't have a fixed soul (*ātman*). Instead, like everything else, I am an ever-changing assemblage of conditions. I learned that I could change in different ways: for 'better' and for 'worse'. I can become not only wiser, kinder, and happier but also more stupid, cruel, and wretched. Moreover, I learned that how I change and what I experience are my responsibility: I reap the fruits of my previous actions, and sow seeds, the fruits of which I will reap in future. This was not only a liberating, but also a frightening insight: I am responsible for my own life, my happiness and unhappiness, and the impact that I have on the world. I can't pass the buck or blame anyone else, but I must face up to how I am creating, even moment by moment, the joy and despair, the love and hatred, and the meaning and futility, that constitute my everyday experience.

As I studied and practised more, these raw insights were placed within the context of more technical Buddhist doctrines. Among the many doctrines I encountered were those of Karma and rebirth. But while I had resonated strongly with the idea that I could change, I found the more formal doctrines less appealing, even alienating. As time went on, I began to feel that the 'ready made' doctrines of the tradition didn't quite 'fit' my experience – like an off-the-peg suit that is too tight round the shoulders or too long in the leg. I realized that – as traditionally presented – at least some of those doctrines didn't fully match my experience of what life is really like. This discovery is not un-common, and can, for some, be worrying, or even undermining, since it shakes their new-found certainty, clarity, and sense of purpose. To avoid this unpleasant sensation, some people may decide to ignore the mismatch and put it down to the fact that their experience is limited. This might well of course be true. Others lose confidence in the teaching and drop their commit-ment to it because it seems inaccurate, perhaps out-of-date, even medieval.

My own aspiration is to engage critically with the doctrines of Buddhism in order to disclose the liberating value that lies within them – if indeed there is any. The fact that they are not a perfect fit doesn't mean they are no use at all; it may simply mean they were designed in very particular circumstances for particular tasks, and they therefore need reinterpretation and adaptation to accurately address my own spiritual condition.

It is common to approach religious doctrines in the same way as we approach everyday statements about experience: we think they are either 'true' or 'not true'. We may think of them as 'mir-rors of nature' that reflect the world back to us exactly as it is in some absolute and ultimate sense. If we accept the doctrines, we tend to cling to them in what may even be an absolute kind of way. We tend to take on the whole package: if this is true then that is probably true too. We become a 'defender of the faith' to which we have subscribed and we may begin to experience criti-cism of it as a personal attack. We invest in the truth of the teach-ings. This can lead us to become dogmatic, defensive, and even aggressive to the point of suppressing or persecuting those who criticize us. At the back of our minds we perhaps sense that not everything we have taken on quite hangs together or makes sense, and this makes us still more rigid in our defence of it. But if a spiritual tradition has any substance, it shouldn't need defending and it will be able to withstand honest scrutiny. If it doesn't, we should probably look for something better.

It seems the Buddha himself was very careful about the kinds of claims he made on behalf of what he had understood and what he therefore taught. He embarked on a very specific project, which he described as teaching about 'suffering and the ending of suffering'. In a famous simile, the Buddha described his Dharma (teaching) as a raft, which could carry us to the farther shore of spiritual awakening.[2] In other words, the Buddha's teachings were pragmatic: they were intended to bring about particular results. In some instances, the Buddha was even willing to use concepts and assumptions clearly tied to non-Buddhist goals in order to foster spiritual development.[3] The raft, then, has a practical, instrumental use: it is a means of transport, not an end in itself.

So in assessing the relevance and value of any particular Buddhist teaching, we need to be attentive to its practical value. How does this teaching help us to progress spiritually? Spiritual teachings evolve in particular circumstances in response to particular problems. The form of the teaching will be expressed in such a way as to address a specific need. Buddhist teachings are not mirrors of nature but more like carefully focused photographs: important foreground details are clearly shown, while the background is often rather hazy. A portrait photographer does not give everything within the field of vision equal value but selects according to the desired composition and effect. In the same way, Buddhist teachings are best understood not as attempts to describe the world 'as it is' in some absolute sense but rather as vistas that enable us to experience our lives in more meaningful, joyful, and creative ways.

Had he been born today the Buddha would have taught differently, perhaps even dramatically differently, because the issues and problems we face today have their own unique features.

Creative intervention in the spiritual challenges of the present requires an approach that takes account of the world-view, psychology, lifestyle, and social structures of the postmodern world, not pretending that the world we live in is more or less the same as that of the ancient Indian. But this does not mean the Buddha's teaching has no enduring value – that it applies only to the India of 500BCE – only that the enduring value may sometimes need liberating from the trappings of an alien cultural vocabulary, some of whose concerns are not ours.

The Buddha is reported to have said that one should test his words like a goldsmith tests gold in the fire.[4] This implies that it is the duty of a rigorously practising Buddhist to test the Buddhist teachings to see whether or not they hold together. We should not tiptoe around them for fear that they might collapse like a house of cards. If the teachings are really that fragile we would be foolish to place our trust in them. Instead, we need vigorously to engage with and test the teachings we encounter, to see if they stack up. Can they withstand serious scrutiny? It will be through vigorous engagement and scrutiny that we will start to dig beneath the surface of a teaching and recover the spiritual treasure that lies buried within it.

To illustrate this, let me use an analogy. At first glance, a coconut may seem a rather weird, exotic thing. It has strange wiry brown hair and makes a rattling noise when shaken. What's inside? Where has it come from? In contemplating this mysterious fruit, this curiosity of the natural world, we could fail to realize that, if we were to break it open, we could actually taste it. To do this, we need to take hold of a hammer and give it a good whack, even to see it splinter into pieces on the kitchen floor. For sure, it might make a mess and we might even feel a sense of loss since the perfect wholeness of the coconut has been destroyed, but it is only now that we can eat it – or discover that actually there is nothing of value inside.

The German theologian Paul Tillich developed the notions of an unbroken myth and a broken myth.[5] An unbroken myth is one that is believed to be true in a literal sense, such as the belief that Christ was literally resurrected in a physical body after his crucifixion and walked along the road at Emmaus.[6] Tillich points out that these days most people are not capable of believing myths in this way without being dishonest to their true thoughts and feelings. Instead, then, we have 'broken' myths, myths which, while not being understood as historical facts, are still held to have deep significance: they are seen as holding truth, value, and meaning but no longer in such a literal sense. So a modern way to understand the Resurrection, for instance, could be more metaphorical and spiritual, wherein, through the arising of faith, Christ becomes resurrected in the heart of the believer.

Richard Holloway, a former Anglican Bishop of Edinburgh, goes further and suggests that instead of 'broken myths' we should think in terms of 'breaking myths open'.[7] On his reading, the meaning of a myth is something hidden, and if we want to taste its fruit we must break through its skin. I believe this approach is also useful in disclosing the spiritual meaning of Buddhist teachings. The traditional doctrines are often embedded in a cultural pattern and cosmology that might seem alien to today's spiritual inquirer. But this does not necessarily mean we should dismiss them. Rather, we need to cut away the bark to reveal the vital heartwood underneath – the transformative value of the Buddha's message.

In this book, I undertake what may seem to some an irreverent, even iconoclastic, investigation of a number of traditional Buddhist teachings in order to unearth what significance they might yield for our unique cultural and historical situation. In some respects my approach is quite personal, for it arises out of intellectual and spiritual difficulties I have experienced in my encounter with traditional Buddhist teachings. I hope, however, that my exploration will resonate with you and, even when you disagree, stimulate you to think more deeply about the issues involved. Rather than offering definitive answers, my aim is to raise questions and to encourage inquiry. As the German philosopher Heidegger writes,

> Questions are paths toward an answer. If the answer could be given it would consist in a transformation of thinking, not in a propositional statement about a matter at stake.[8]

1

INTRODUCING
KARMA & REBIRTH

Human existence is a strange thing. It seems at once miraculous, wonderful, bizarre, and frightening. We awake to find ourselves thrown into a world that we don't understand but for which we want – even need – an explanation, a map with which to navigate through this weird territory. Why are we here? Where did we come from? What is this place? What will happen when we die? The fact that we can interrogate our lives and ask what they mean and where we are heading is itself a deeply strange, even unsettling, thing. Like aliens waking on a foreign planet and suffering from amnesia, we try to piece together a story that we call our lives and a scenario that we call the world. We follow clues, write things down, and try to remember who we are and what we are supposed to be doing. Like the central character in the film *Memento*,[9] who has lost his short-term memory, we draw together scraps of seeming significance, only to find that the fragile story we have stitched together can be broken open in a moment. In an effort to make sense of the mystery that confronts us, we don't tattoo notes on to our bodies – like the character in the film – but etch them into our minds, and put together a story that makes some sense of the mystery that is our life.

In the course of our journey across this strange planet, we encounter other beings. Very soon we realize that most of them are not like us; people are marked out from each other by many differences: in colour, language, culture, intelligence, wealth, and so on. We discover that some children are born with nothing in their mouths, others with silver spoons. Our televisions and newspapers show us how some are born into war-torn lands rent by famine, floods, and earthquakes, while others enjoy a peaceful state where food is plentiful and disasters are rare. On hearing of the latest floods in Mozambique, or the latest earthquake in India, it is hard not to think that some people have been marked out for disaster. Some people's lives are tragedies, while others build success upon success and everything comes easily to them; some suffer disasters while fortune seems to smile on others. If we are even a little curious, we must be tempted to ask why; who and what is responsible for this? Surely there must be some method in the stark inequalities that divide the rich and the poor, the blessed and the wretched? There must be some way of explaining why the world is so unfair.

Is it God? Is it fate? Is it destined from the beginning? Are our lives bound to follow a predetermined course? Is there some divine principle that intervenes in our lives to shape our destinies? Or is it simply luck, chance, a random distribution of lots good and bad? Or are we perhaps simply getting what we deserve? Life doesn't seem to be even-handed towards everyone; this much seems clear. But how is this reality, which seems so fickle and so unfair, to be understood and explained?

It would seem that the human heart has a deep need for answers to such questions. We might even suggest that the provision of satisfying explanations for such inequalities is an essential function of religion. The question of why fortune does not favour all has certainly preoccupied religious thinkers down the ages. In the early Buddhist scriptures, Subha, the son of an eminent Brahman, puts such a question to the Buddha.[10] Subha wants to know why some people are rich and others poor, why some are long-lived and others short-lived, some ugly and others beautiful, some stupid and others wise. In short, he wants an explanation of inequality. The Buddha's reported response is very succinct:

> Student, beings are owners of their actions (*karmas*), heirs of their actions; they originate from their actions, are bound to their actions, have their actions as their refuge. It is action that distinguishes beings as inferior and superior.[11]

This famous dictum introduces the Buddhist teaching on Karma. But what sense can we make of it? While the word *karma* (literally, 'action') is now part of everyday English, its meaning is often left rather vague. Roughly put, Karma is a moral principle that governs human conduct. It declares that our present experience is conditioned by our past conduct and that our present conduct will condition our future experience. This might seem pretty obvious, but most readings of Karma go quite a bit further than this. Before presenting my own working definition of Karma, I will give a brief summary of some of the prevailing ideas so that the issues might be laid out more clearly.

First of all, Karma is often equated with the general Buddhist principle of dependent origination (*pratītya samutpāda*). It is regarded as 'the master Law of the Universe,'[12] the law of causation. In Chapter 3, we will see how this reading conflates an *instance* of the Buddhist teaching of dependent origination with the general principle itself. This confusion results in a muddled understanding of how and why things happen as they do, which has become embodied in the misleading view that moral forces determine all outcomes.

Secondly, Karma is often presented as a principle of moral equilibrium that restores balance and harmony in the universe.[13] So if I act badly in some way, then, sooner or later, some bad thing will inevitably happen to me since this is necessary in order to 'rebalance' the universe. On this understanding, our actions must be seen as almost mechanical transactions with definite values that have equal and even commensurate paybacks.

Karma is also described as a 'retributive' principle, an 'iron law' underlying a 'just' universe that punishes wrongdoers and rewards the virtuous. So if anything bad happens to us it *must* be because we ourselves have done something, either earlier in this life or in a previous one, to have 'deserved' it. Similarly, if we receive any reward or good fortune it *must* be because we have acted well in the past. While describing Karma as a retributive principle is not altogether wrong, it can be misleading because it implies that Karma is a sort of cosmic judge, perhaps even an intelligent force, dispassionately handing out appropriate punishments and rewards. It also implies that *all* fortune and misfortune is best accounted for by means of personal moral strengths and failings. So, on this reading, no sufferings are unwarranted and no blessings unearned. This is a view that I will call into question.

Finally, Karma is seen by some as a principle of inevitability akin to fate, which suggests that things are simply 'destined' to happen. So if, for instance, my car gets stolen that is my karma, if I win the lottery that is my karma, if I get abducted by aliens then that is my karma too. But what does it mean to say that something is my karma? This is not at all clear. It can seem like a facile response to an unexpected and unwelcome eventuality. In what sense these events are 'supposed to happen', and are fitting, is less than obvious, and explanations are rarely offered. One of the limitations of such judgements is that they are always made r the event; there is no means of verifying or disproving them. With hindsight we can always see that 'we had it coming'.

Such readings can result in an understanding of Karma as a mystical law whose operation it is impossible to fathom but which mysteriously guides the course of events. If objections are raised, appeal can be made to the ineffable nature of the law. This means that belief in Karma becomes an article of faith, rather than something to be understood through experience. This results in two difficulties. First, if one is convinced that Karma is true in the ways described above, no amount of reasonable objections or apparent contradictions are likely to cause one to doubt it. Secondly, if one does not have faith it becomes difficult to acquire, because one is unlikely to accept that a moral cause lies behind an event (such as a meteor strike) that can easily be explained without it. I want to propose that Karma is not at all mysterious but part and parcel of ordinary, everyday life. We don't need special mystical powers to understand how it works, just a little common-sense reflection. It is a human law, the influence of which is to be seen in the day-to-day decisions we make about our lives.

In this book, Karma will be understood as a principle that shows how morally-guided conduct (which includes thoughts) impacts upon oneself, other people, and the world. First of all, through our intentional conduct, we transform who we are: we become what we do, say, and think. Secondly, this conduct influences – but doesn't determine – how others think and act in relation to us. Thirdly, it results in our own unique experience of the world; in a sense, it creates our world. For instance, whether we experience the world as fearful or pleasurable is a product of our karma. This way of understanding Karma is primarily psychological, as opposed to what could be described as the cosmological accounts outlined above.

But in offering the above definition we are perhaps jumping the gun. As we shall see, there are several different Karma doctrines belonging to distinct Indian religious traditions, while even within Buddhism itself there is no obvious definitive understanding of it. Despite this, I think our starting point does at least some justice to Karma as traditionally conceived and understood, as well as taking account of modern ways of understanding the world.

Within Buddhism, the principle of Karma has been inextricably linked with the notion of rebirth or re-becoming (*punarbhava*). This doctrine asserts that when we die we will be born again, not in eternal heaven or hell but in a new physical body consistent with the degree of moral goodness we have expressed in our present life (and sometimes previous lives). The Buddhist tradition has elaborated a detailed cosmology to explain what sort of rebirth we might expect, given particular moral strengths or failings. Importantly, the process of birth, death, and rebirth (*saṃsāra*) is said to continue indefinitely until we become spiritually liberated. We shall learn more of this later.

But what sense can we make of this notion of rebirth? To many Westerners, educated within the materialistic paradigm of modern science, rebirth may seem a rather naive, even primitive, belief (which does not, of course, mean it is wrong or useless). Upon what grounds does Buddhism base its claims for the reality of rebirth? How does rebirth happen? Is it to be taken literally or is it better understood as a myth, the meaning of which is more symbolic? Can the concept of Karma have any meaning without an associated notion of rebirth? These are some of the questions I intend to look at.

In what follows, we will engage critically with some traditional accounts of Karma and rebirth doctrines. We will learn how Buddhist understandings of these doctrines evolved from earlier Indian religion, which led to a certain degree of confusion and inconsistency within Buddhism itself. My objective is not so much to prove whether they are true or false but rather to understand whether and in what ways they can function as credible beliefs that serve a useful spiritual function. I suggest that in order to lead an effective spiritual life we need a set of beliefs and practices that motivate us to positively transform ourselves. The issue, then, is not whether or not we believe but, rather, *how* does what we believe influence how we live? This type of self-audit can be extended further: how do *all* our beliefs and views influence our actions? Does what we believe about the world enable us to live more creatively? If not, should we change something? In following this approach, I suggest we need to be wary of measuring our spiritual integrity or 'holiness' in terms of how much traditional doctrine we are able to agree with. Self-transformation, not assent to religious doctrines, is the goal of spiritual life. The effective Buddhist is one who consciously engages with spiritual beliefs in order to determine how they might promote awareness, ethical sensitivity, and creative engagement with life.

2

THE ORIGINS OF
KARMA & REBIRTH

It would be naive to assume that the notions of Karma and rebirth emerged fully developed, like revelations, through the
Buddha's ministry; doctrines rarely appear so dramatically.
Ideas require nourishment and favourable conditions in order to
mature. Doctrines gestate within a broad cultural context of
ideas and practices and often evolve as direct responses to specific issues and difficulties. They may even develop *in opposition*
to prevailing ideas, and this is true of some important features of
the Buddhist account of Karma and rebirth. Even if the Buddha's spiritual awakening was genuinely new, he had to refer to
prevailing religious ideas in order to express it. He may have had
some new wine, but he had to put it in the old bottles. So if we
are to understand the issues that Buddhist accounts of Karma
and rebirth were concerned to address, we need to learn more
about their cultural and religious background.

Karma and Rebirth Before the Buddha
The mother culture that gave birth to Buddhism was dominated
by Brahmanical thought and practice. Brahmanism took

inspiration and guidance from orally revealed texts, especially the Vedas but later also the Upanishads. The concepts of Karma and rebirth developed gradually, materializing from little more than a shadowy presence in the Vedas to a clearer definition in some of the Upanishads. Buddhism significantly developed its own thought *in relation* to the Brahmanical, both positively and negatively. Positively, Buddhism accepted a number of key terms and religious themes as providing a paradigm for the spiritual life; negatively, it rejected some leading Brahmanical ideas such as the *ātman* (eternal soul). Three main ideas formed the core of this new religious paradigm, which was to define the pattern of later spiritual traditions within India. These were *saṃsāra* (the endless round), Karma, and *mokṣa* (liberation).[14]

The religious life of Brahmanism focused on the ritual sacrifice, which played a magical role in the life of the cosmos. Sacrifice was needed to prolong time, which did not exist independently but was created and sustained by the sacrifices themselves. The gods sustained the cosmos and the life of the gods was prolonged through continual rebirth owing to the sacrifices made by the Brahmans. As with the gods, the life of man had to be sustained, but unlike them man would inevitably die at the end of his natural span.

While human existence after death is referred to only vaguely in the Vedas, a later group of texts called the Brāhmaṇas describes a more clearly defined afterlife. Sacrifice now came to be understood as a means by which to ensure rebirth in a god-like realm (*devaloka*) after death: if one properly conducted the necessary rituals, the 'merit' (*puñña*) gained from them could be transferred to one's after-death state and sustain life in the *devaloka*. Thus emerged the notion of a world of sacrificial merit, where those who had earned the rewards of well-performed rites would go after death. Rebirth in the *devaloka* was determined by ritual efficiency: as yet it had little to do with ethics. In

accordance with a system of correspondences, correctly performed rituals were believed to have a magical power that left a
residue of merit which *automatically* produced future benefits
for the person making the sacrifice.[15] The sacrifice created a kind
of karmic deposit bond that could be cashed in posthumously.[16]

At this stage it was still believed that life in the *deva* realm
would eventually run out, resulting in a final death. This led to
the development of the idea that this death meant an inevitable
return to life on earth and consequently the notion of *saṃsāra;*
the endless round of birth, death, and rebirth. The *Chandogya
Upanishad* goes as far as offering the possibility of different kinds
of rebirths depending upon one's conduct.[17] *All* actions could
now be seen as important in relation to one's afterlife, not just
special rituals.

The notion of sacrifice was later internalized in the life of the
renunciant who went forth from village and family to live a life
of asceticism in the forest, with no permanent home, and often
begging for food. The entire life of the ascetic became a kind of
sacrificial performance, which brought positive rewards in the
afterlife. This expression of spirituality continued to rely primarily on a ritualistic notion of action rather than a moral one; the
spiritual life was seen in terms of specific kinds of ascetic acts,
such as deliberately burning oneself, rather than the development of virtues. While the ascetic lifestyle was also to dominate
early Buddhist practice, its meaning was significantly revised.

Ascetics got up to all sorts of weird activities in the belief that
they would thereby be liberated. For instance, in one early dialogue the Buddha encounters a couple of wanderers, one whose
practice consisted in behaving like a dog, the other in mimicking
an ox.[18] They ask the Buddha what their future birth is likely to
be. At first he seems reluctant to answer, but in what seems to be
a light-hearted moment, the Buddha replies that if they practise
assiduously they may hope to be reborn as a dog and an ox

respectively, but if they don't, they will be reborn in hell. Although this might seem a little harsh, it illustrates how - from the Buddhist point of view - this kind of asceticism was considered ridiculous and irrelevant.

The Buddha seems to have been the first spiritual leader to work out a thoroughly ethicized notion of Karma.[19] For him, it wasn't enough to perform a prescribed ritual in the proper manner or to undertake the appropriate bizarre ascetic act; what was fundamentally important was the *mental attitude* – or volition – that motivated the action. The Buddha came to see all morally charged actions as significant in relation to one's future life and one's afterlife. Exactly how this worked we shall see later.

This shift from the significance of external performance to the significance of underlying intention is brought out in a text called the *Upāli Sutta*, in which the Buddha debates with a Jain practitioner.[20] Jainism was a rival spiritual tradition which emerged around the same time as Buddhism. In this text, the Buddha asks Dīgha Tapassī which mode of action is the most reprehensible for the performance of evil conduct: body, speech, or mind (a traditional threefold division). The Jain replies that bodily action is obviously the most reprehensible. In Jain philosophy, karma was seen as a kind of dust that adhered to the soul, weighing it down and preventing it rising to heaven. The objective was to free the soul from its karmic accretions, and this was to be achieved by adopting a policy of extreme *inaction* in order to avoid harming living beings since, for the Jains, it was primarily physical conduct that created karma. This has led some Jains to go to extreme measures, such as wearing a mask to avoid inhaling insects and sweeping the path ahead of them so as not to crush any creature underfoot.

When asked himself which mode of action is the most reprehensible, the Buddha replies that it is mental action. This discussion is reported to Nigaṇṭha Nātaputta, the leader of the Jain

sect, and Upāli, one of his leading disciples, offers to go and debate this with the Buddha. Upāli cockily declares that just as a
strong man would grab hold of a long-haired ram by the hair
and drag him to and fro and round about, so, in debate, will he
drag the Buddha. Needless to say, it does not take long for the
Buddha to convert Upāli to his own position. Though presented
in a highly stylized form, this dialogue illustrates the clash of
two distinct approaches to ethics. For the Jains, karma was primarily a matter of external behaviour, whereas for the Buddha it
was the underlying intention that most counted. This internal-
ization of ethics is fundamental to understanding the meaning
of Karma within Buddhism.

Continuities with Earlier Tradition

Although it made some significant changes to prevailing notions
of Karma, Buddhism nevertheless adopted the core ideas of
Brahmanism concerning man's place in the cosmic scheme, as
well as its key terms for articulating the framework for spiritual
life. So the Buddha continued to define the human predicament
in terms of *saṃsāra*, and it was precisely this that gave human life
its unsatisfactory quality. He also defined the goal of the religious life in terms of escaping from it, thus developing the earlier notion of *mokṣa* (liberation). Since Karma came to be seen as
the mechanism by which the individual continued on through
the cycle of birth and death, the spiritual goal would consist in
breaking free of the workings of Karma. The Buddha called this
condition Nirvāṇa, which literally means 'extinguished', or
'blown out', as a flame.

Not only did Brahmanism and Jainism have their own distinctive understanding of Karma and rebirth, but even *within*
Buddhism there has been considerable diversity of opinion on
many aspects of these doctrines. All these ideas grew from a

common soil. While it can be tempting for the spiritually committed person to think that the doctrines and teachings they have adopted are unique revelations, this may be to ignore their strong resemblance to ideas that preceded them. But to recognize that a teaching has emerged from a cultural context need not be to reduce or dismiss it; in learning about how the new teaching developed or departed from earlier ones, we can learn what is distinctive about it. A spiritual teaching doesn't stand or fall on its uniqueness but on its transformative value.

The Legacy of Pre-Buddhist Ideas

While the religious paradigm and the leading themes of religious life were not only adopted but also profitably adapted by the Buddhist tradition, this process also created anomalies. Anyone who has been involved in the conversion of an old building knows that the purpose, design, and construction of the original will influence the final appearance. Between 1995 and 1997, I was involved in a project to restore and convert a former cotton warehouse in Manchester. Our aim was to create an urban Buddhist centre. When we had finished, anyone walking through the building would have been forgiven for wondering why we chose to make the rooms such strange shapes and why the corridors were so narrow. The answer is that the original design of the building – which was a kind of Z-shape – restricted the changes we could undertake. Religious ideas are often 'converted' in an analogous way.

Perhaps the main legacy of pre-Buddhist notions of Karma and rebirth was confusion: what did Karma really mean in the context of the Buddha's teaching? How did the process work? The early scriptures themselves seem inconsistent in their interpretation of Karma, and this probably reflects not only a diversity of opinion but also a process of gradual development.

For instance, some notions of Karma prevalent in the Buddha's time saw it as the cause of everything that happens.[21] From this it was thought to follow that one's social position (or caste) resulted from one's conduct in a previous life. The recommended means of purifying one's previous karma was to discharge one's caste duty; whether that was to function as a religious instructor (Brahman) or to carry out low status 'polluting' jobs such as cleaning toilets (the so-called 'Untouchables'). Change of status and position within one's current life was believed impossible; one should instead prepare the conditions for a higher caste rebirth by following one's allotted role. This belief was reflected in a rigid social system of caste (any movement within which was strictly forbidden), a system that, while not legally sanctioned, is still in force even today.

According to this view, Karma is a kind of moral feedback loop, a system of universal and inescapable retribution. All the pain we experience is a direct consequence of our previous evil conduct; there can be no undeserved suffering. At the same time, all the benefits we receive are due to our past good deeds. One of the main limitations of this way of thinking about Karma and rebirth is that this is untestable and unfalsifiable. If someone claims that everything that happens to us is a result of our karma, there is no decisive way of disproving this, however unlikely it may seem and however more plausible are other explanations. But because we cannot conclusively disprove it does not mean we must accept it. We need to ask whether it is useful to think in this way. An example will show some of the limitations of an approach that understands everything to be the result of one's past good or bad deeds.

Let us say that the roof of my house falls in. If I assume that this must be because I have done something bad in a past life, I will perhaps respond to this event by redoubling my efforts to lead an ethical life. This is all well and good. However, if I have the roof replaced just as it was before and it falls in again, I am likely to think that I am reaping further consequences of my past evil. But if, instead of imputing a moral cause for the collapse of the roof, I assume it is the result of a construction fault, I will remedy the fault. This example aims to show that, in at least some cases, attributing moral causes to external events leads to inappropriate responses.

But there is a further difficulty with the kind of account of Karma we have sketched out. It undermines the principle of free will and tends in the direction of moral determinism. This issue is tackled directly by the Buddha:

> There are certain recluses and brāhmins who teach thus, who hold this view: – Whatsoever weal or woe or neutral feeling is experienced, all that is due to some previous action.... Then I say to them: 'So then, owing to a previous action, men will become murderers, thieves, unchaste, liars, slanderers, abusive, babblers, covetous, malicious, and perverse in view. Thus for those who fall back on the former deed as the essential reason there is neither desire to do, nor effort to do, nor necessity to do this deed or abstain from that deed.[22]

The Buddha goes on to point out that such a view precludes the possibility of the spiritual life, since such a life requires the possibility that we can change for the better; if we are entirely governed by our past actions this is impossible.

Likewise, if the way in which others act towards us is purely a result of our karma, are they free to act differently? For instance, if I get off with another guy's girlfriend at a party, and as a result he is so jealous and angry that he intends to give me a good beating, you may think I deserve it. But what if one of his friends calms him down and dissuades him from reacting violently? Is this consequence – which seems very positive for me – purely a result of my previous karma? What the strictly 'feedback' interpretation of Karma seems to miss out is that the way in which others respond to us is not determined solely by our actions; depending on their own character, they might respond in a number of different ways. It would seem strange, then, to think that their response is determined by our karma alone. While our own actions usually influence how others respond to us, they don't always. A saint, for instance, may be willing to help an evil person as much as a good one (perhaps even more willing).

If everything that happens to us is a result of our previous karma, then one could say that we suffer for a reason, we are meant to suffer, the universe is teaching us a lesson. This might seem to be a creative response, but the danger is that we may come to think that we should simply endure our suffering rather than attempt to release ourselves from it, because, by doing so, our previous karma will be 'purified'. Such an outlook can undermine the value of much charitable work. Since people are in dire straits owing to their previous conduct, we should not interfere because this would adversely affect the working out of their karma. If we intervened now they would only have to suffer later on. This may go some way to explain why efforts at social welfare and uplift of the poor have not been high priorities in India. On the whole, people have tended to accept their lot rather than to think about changing it.

While it is common for today's Buddhists to deny that Buddhism attributes everything that happens in our lives to Karma, there are early scriptures that seem to put forward a view of this kind[23] and it has become the orthodox view within Tibetan Buddhism. Given the ferment of ideas that characterized the Buddha's time, it is hardly surprising that the Buddhist view is not uniform. But even while some scriptural passages can be found that seem to indicate that everything that happens to us is governed by Karma, there are many others which state very clearly that this is not the case.

In the *Devadaha Sutta*,[24] for instance, the Buddha encounters a group of Jain ascetics. The Jains believed that through asceticism they would annihilate the consequences of their past actions and become purified. The Buddha dismisses this approach and admonishes them for heaping further suffering upon them-selves unnecessarily. He rejects the view that all the pleasure and pain we experience results from previous conduct.[25] The Buddha also denies that deliberately imposed suffering can be an effective means of 'burning off' past karma, while recogniz-ing that a certain amount of suffering may result from struggling against one's spiritual limitations. He likened this situation to an arrowsmith who heats an arrow to make it workable. This meta-phor shows us how in the course of spiritual practice we may encounter a degree of suffering as part of our path towards tran-scending it, but that such suffering is not 'spiritual', only unavoidable. Crucially, we should not consciously prolong or intensify suffering in the belief that it will result in spiritual benefits. It won't.

We have already seen that a further legacy of pre-Buddhist notions of Karma was that karmas had come to be widely under-stood as transactions that yielded prescribed positive or nega-tive merit. This had led to the notion that merit was 'held in trust' to be reaped in the afterlife or in future lives, or could even be transferred to another individual. Some Buddhist accounts of Karma seem never to have fully shaken off this commodified understanding of Karma and merit, which encouraged a some-what mechanical – rather than an ethical – approach to conduct.

For instance, in Sri Lanka when someone dies it is usual for the relatives to make an offering (of food) to the local monks and for the 'merit' of the act of giving to be 'transferred' to the departed relative. This practice and the belief that underlies it seem to contradict the basic Buddhist principle of self-responsibility, and imply that merit is a kind of property that can be given away to ameliorate the negative effects of Karma, a possibility Buddhism usually denies. As the *Dhammapada* says,

> A man besmirches himself by the evil he personally commits. (Similarly) he purifies himself by personally abstaining from evil. Purity and impurity are matters of personal experience: one man cannot purify another.[16]

With regard to rebirth, Buddhism inherited other problems. As a doctrine, rebirth had evolved in conjunction with the view that living beings all have an eternal self (*ātman*). Given that one of the primary Buddhist teachings is that all things are impermanent, this must also apply to human beings. The problem for Buddhism then became: if there is no fixed self what is it that is reborn? Is it our memories? Is it our habits? How could these be transferred from one being to another? The Buddhist tradition generated a whole host of new doctrines, some highly bizarre, in order to resolve this apparent difficulty. It is arguably a question that has never been satisfactorily answered.

Finally, rebirth has generally been regarded as one of the central tenets of Buddhism. Its function has been largely coercive; it is held up as a frightener in order to shake practitioners into better conduct. For Buddhism, rebirth has been an undesirable but unavoidable religious fact. It is questionable whether it can retain this function when transposed into Western cultural experience. Many Westerners would regard rebirth as a desirable, rather than a disagreeable, proposition. Does it, then, aid effective practice? Or could it encourage complacency? Are there any ways in which it can be meaningfully understood within the context of our Western experience? These questions will be taken up later.

3

KARMA AND DEPENDENT ORIGINATION

The Buddhist understanding of Karma and rebirth should be seen in the light of the Buddha's most fundamental insight, as expressed through the doctrine of 'dependent origination'. Dependent origination is an all-embracing principle that *includes* Karma but is not limited to it; the two should not be conflated. According to this teaching, all things arise in dependence upon conditions; when those conditions cease, the thing itself ceases. So, for instance, a tree lives and grows in dependence on soil, air, sunshine, and rain. Without a vast range of supporting conditions, the tree will wither and die. But we tend to look at things in isolation, thinking of them as independent of their surroundings and having a core that carries on through time. This is particularly the case with objects. In order to prevent our experience from being just a chaotic jumble, we need to name things: house, car, bird, and so on. But we then go on to assume that there really is a 'thing' to which that name corresponds. So, for example, we come up with the name 'sky' and then assume that there really is a 'thing' that corresponds to that word.

For everyday purposes this approach works fine; we need to be able to distinguish, classify, and conceptualize in order to navigate through life, just as a sailor needs a map to cross the sea. But the map does not mirror the sea. If we look at any natural phenomenon, it is not only constantly changing but its very existence depends on a huge number of factors, far more than we can normally take into consideration. Forgetting that the map is something by which to navigate, the unawakened mind believes it to be a perfect reflection of the sea, providing a complete and accurate description of how the sea *really* is. While no mariner would seek to launch his ship on the map, the unawakened mind rests its most important beliefs on its *model* of experience rather than experience itself. This mistake leads not only to confusion but also to suffering.

According to the Buddha, our way of thinking about the world (our map) leads us to think of things – including ourselves – as permanent, and this results in suffering once experience shows us that they are not. For instance, we might enter into marriage believing it will last for ever, but a few years later we find ourselves divorced, lonely, and distraught. Dependent origination encourages us to view our experience more in terms of a constantly changing process rather than a static state of affairs. This means that even while things grow, develop, and improve they can also decay, die, and fall apart. Positively, dependent origination means that we can develop a loving relationship, but negatively it means that the very same relationship can disintegrate into hostility and hatred and end in heartbreak. The Buddha encouraged people to think of all experience as impermanent: if the conditions that support it start to break down, our relationship will disintegrate. A deep understanding of this insight can lead us to a serene withdrawal from attachment to mundane things: since ultimately they are unreliable we shouldn't expect too much of them. That all things are impermanent is also a truth that applies to us: *we* are impermanent. Not only will we die but there is nothing within us that is fixed and unchangeable; there is no core, no soul that will continue eternally. We are neither condemned to carry on as we are – we can change – nor will we live for ever.

Later Buddhist philosophy sees the universe as an interconnected whole; any condition is understood to be dependent for its subsistence on *all* other conditions (though some conditions are more immediately important than others) because everything is in dynamic interaction with everything else. The universe, experience, is an indivisible whole; if we change one thing we change everything, however subtly. Traditionally, the miraculous image of Indra's jewelled net is used to illustrate this.[7] In each and every jewel of which the net is composed, all the other jewels are reflected such that each jewel is reflected in all and all in each. By meditating on this magical image, we can begin to open our imagination to the mysterious beauty of the Buddhist vision of reality.

The principle of dependent origination can be applied to any phenomenon: the natural world, politics, the cosmos, human relationships, and the human individual. It is the most generalized way of describing everything that happens. But some Buddhist teachers, and even Buddhist schools, conflate Karma with the more general principle and so believe that it governs everything. This is a dangerous misunderstanding. A crude version of the Karma doctrine makes it responsible for all the triumphs and tragedies of life: if we get shipwrecked then that is somehow a working out of our karma; if a brick falls on our head as we walk down the street, that's our karma; if our family is killed in a plane crash, that's our karma; if we win the National Lottery, well, that's our good karma. This kind of understanding of Karma is found, for example, in Tibetan Buddhism. The Tibetans seem to believe that everything that happens to us is a result of our previous karma. For example, when interviewing Lati Rimpoche, Richard Hayes asked him whether he believed that all the Jews who were gassed by the Germans in the Second World War deserved their deaths. Rimpoche replied:

> The victims were experiencing the consequences of their actions performed in previous lives. The individual victims must have done something very bad in earlier lives that led to their being treated in this way.[28]

It may be unwise to state categorically that the Rimpoche must be wrong but, whether they were meant as such or not, his words can be read as an explanation of the events of the holocaust. The Rimpoche's insistence that the Jews must have done something very bad in a previous life suggests that he believes that all suffering, even that as horrific as the Nazi death camps, is at least in part, if not completely, a consequence of previous misbehaviour. It would easily follow that the Jews 'deserved' their fate. As we will soon see, such a point of view is not in harmony with the early Buddhist scriptures. More importantly, though, is this a useful way of thinking? In the minds of many, such an explanation could all too easily result in callousness, as well as a lessening of the liability of the Nazis. Not only this, but if we think that people in some sense deserve their suffering, we might be tempted to become passive and not intervene to alleviate their misery; after all, they are getting what is coming to them.

If it were true that the Jews were being punished, then remarkable survival stories such as that of the Schindler Jews would be difficult to account for.[29] Presumably they must have survived because of their good karma from previous lives. If you are curious like me, you may find all sorts of questions now springing to mind. How, for instance, did Schindler know which Jews he was supposed to select for survival? Presumably he didn't consciously know, so is it being suggested that some invisible power (Karma) somehow acted through him, guiding his decisions so that he saved the 'right' Jews? Would this mean that he could not have acted differently? Could he have chosen Jews who didn't 'deserve' to be saved? Could he have chosen to save no one at all? Contorted explanations can no doubt be found to account for all this, but the point is, surely, whether views such as these help us guide our actions wisely and compassionately.

We have already seen that the Buddha did not see anything inherently spiritual about suffering. Since there would seem to be no way of verifying whether the Jews suffered as a result of their evil conduct in previous lives, what use does it serve to think like this? We would all surely agree that the most important thing is to alleviate suffering no matter how it arises. It is interesting to note here that the practice of Tibetan Buddhism – far from being callous and cold – emphasizes the importance of compassion, a profound human response to the suffering of others that is not governed by just deserts. At least at first glance, its view on Karma would appear to contradict this emphasis on compassion.

Returning to the Schindler example, it seems important to insist that the Nazis and Schindler himself made their own choices, choices that were not solely determined by the karmic legacy of the Jews, and that they therefore bear personal responsibility for their actions. Unless we can insist on this, we would seem condemned to a fatalistic view of life and so to entrapment in a world in which no one can choose freely, but in which, instead, everything that anyone does to us is simply a result of our karma and everything that we do to them is a result of theirs. This way of thinking ultimately leads to a kind of solipsism: other people only appear to make free decisions, in reality they are agents of our karma. The universe becomes a neatly interlocking moral jigsaw in which there is no spontaneity, no generosity, only just deserts. Such a view is a long way from core Buddhist teachings.

This retributive approach to understanding why some people suffer while others thrive perhaps has a psychological root: the universe *must* be just. Surely 'innocent' people don't suffer arbitrarily? It might seem very difficult to accept, but perhaps they do. To conflate Karma with the more general principle of dependent origination is to misunderstand Buddhist doctrine. Karma is only a particular application of the general principle to a very restricted range of occurrences, that is, willed human actions. It follows then that to account for all personal suffering by referring *solely* to conduct in a past life is likely to result in a distorted view.

Another lama encourages us to 'see the pain we are going through as the completion of the effects, the fruition, of a past karma.'[30] This statement may be read somewhat differently from that of Lati Rimpoche. Here we could engage in a kind of thought experiment. We could act 'as if' the pain we are experiencing is a result of our previous evil. The value of this is that we might then be able to endure our suffering with greater equanimity. *Sorrow Mountain*, the record of Ani Pachen, provides a moving example of this way of thinking.[31] Ani Pachen was a Tibetan chieftainess who was arrested, imprisoned, and horrifically mistreated by the Chinese. Throughout her many years of torture and deprivation she reflected that she must have done terrible things in her previous lives to be treated in such an appalling way. She describes being savagely beaten by Chinese guards who lashed her face, hands, back, and feet with sticks:

> My ears were beginning to ring, and my face was burning.
> My previous karma, I thought. The pain will eliminate my
> sins.[32]

While there may be a pragmatic value in seeing certain events in our own lives as the outcome of previous karma, it seems, at the same time, extremely dangerous to extend such reflection to

others and conclude that the sufferings *they* experience are a result of their previous evil conduct and we may run the risk of
abdicating responsibility for our own conduct. For instance, two
surgeons recently performed an operation on a man to remove a
failing kidney but removed his healthy one by mistake. He died
shortly afterwards.[33] Was the failure to remove the correct kidney a result of the man's previous evil conduct, or was it primarily a result of the carelessness of the surgeons? If we conclude it
was the man's previous karma then what responsibility do the
surgeons bear for their fatal error? What seems most important
here is for the surgeons to be held to account. Reference to past
lives seems rather wild speculation here. While it is conceivable
that the karma of both the 'victim' and the surgeons influenced
this tragic outcome, the commonly espoused Tibetan view
seems committed to seeing the event as mainly – even completely – a result of the victim's previous actions.

In addition to the reasons already given, taking what seems
like an absolute responsibility for everything bad (as well as
good) that happens to us is particularly unhelpful in the
post-Christian West. Many people feel deeply guilty and negative about themselves owing to the influence of Christian teachings about original sin, even when they have consciously
rejected those teachings. A message that says we suffer because
we have done bad things in previous lives may just reinforce this
negative self-evaluation and encourage despair and self-
loathing. This is not spiritually helpful. Instead, a more creative
response would be to identify areas of life in which suffering can
be overcome and then to develop strategies that alleviate it.

If we attribute everything that befalls us to the workings of
Karma, and we see Karma as a principle of reward and retribution, it would follow that we deserve everything we get and
should accept it with good grace, since we will thereby purify
our past karma. This thinking has underpinned the horrors of

the caste system within Hinduism for centuries. But can we sub-scribe to the view that indiscriminate disasters such as famine, typhoons, and earthquakes are all expressions of Karma?

In October 2002, an earthquake struck a small village in Italy, completely destroying the local schoolhouse.[34] Few other build-ings were seriously damaged. More than two dozen people were killed, almost all of whom were children, but at least the same number were rescued. Was it the children's karma that some were killed and others survived? It would seem extremely prob-lematic to use personal moral strengths or failings to explain the impact of such an unpredictable event, the consequences of which are contingent upon an enormous number of factors. The number of available rescuers and how effectively trained they are will, for instance, have an impact on how many people sur-vive such a situation.

An unwelcome outcome of seeing all disasters as karmic results is that this may invite passivity; if everyone is simply reaping the fruit of their previous karma, then why intervene? After all, if we cut short someone's present suffering, won't they have to suffer again in future until they 'burn off' their karma? Thinking like this could have the perverse effect of discouraging us from acting compassionately towards others, yet this is a fundamental aim of Buddhism. Everyone is worthy of *mettā* (loving-kindness) whatever they have done; it is not a reward for good conduct but an affirmation of their humanity and their potential for spiritual growth.

The Five Modes of Dependent Origination

There is a very important but little known Pali scripture called the *Moliyasīvaka Sutta* in which the Buddha is asked whether he accepts the view that all suffering and all pleasure are caused by previous conduct. The Buddha's reply is very clear:

> When those ascetics and brahmins hold such a doctrine
> and view as this, 'Whatever a person experiences, whether
> it be pleasant or painful or neither-painful-nor-pleasant, all
> that is caused by what was done in the past,' they overshoot
> what one knows by oneself and they overshoot what is con-
> sidered to be true in the world. Therefore I say that this is
> wrong on the part of those ascetics and brahmins.[35]

The text goes on to outline a number of other causes for pleasurable, painful, and neutral feeling, of which Karma is just one.[36]
These include physical illnesses and the influence of the environment. The same issue is tackled in an early Buddhist work
called the *Milindapañha* or 'Questions of King Milinda'.[37] Among
many other thorny questions, the king asks Nāgasena, a Buddhist monk, how feelings of pleasure and pain arise. In summariz-
ing the teaching given in the *Moliyasīvaka Sutta*, Nāgasena
makes it clear that not all feeling has its root in karma. He
concludes,

> Whoever says, 'It is only *kamma* that oppresses beings,' … is
> wrong.… The pain which is due to *kamma* is much less than
> that due to other causes. The ignorant go too far when they
> say that everything that is experienced is produced as the
> fruit of *kamma*. Without a Buddha's insight no one can as-
> certain the extent of the action of *kamma*.[38]

While the schema outlined in the *Moliyasīvaka Sutta* is a bit
obscure, Buddhist scholastic philosophy (known as Abhi-
dhamma) classified five modes – technically known as *niyamas* –
of dependent origination[39] (see fig. 1). These modes are (1) physical inorganic (*utu-niyama*), (2) biological (*bīja-niyama*), (3)
non-volitional mental (*mano- or citta-niyama*), (4) ethical (*kamma-
or karma-niyama*), and (5) spiritual (*dhamma- or dharma-niyama*).

Examination of these *niyamas* can give us a better understanding of the scope and importance of Karma in human life. The

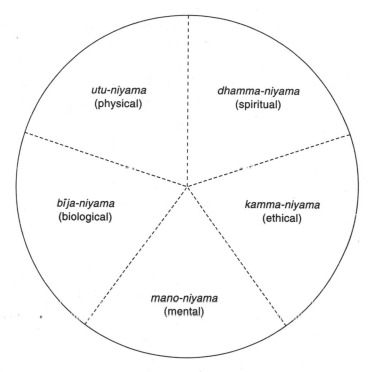

FIG. 1: THE FIVE MODES (NIYAMAS) OF DEPENDENT ORIGINATION

utu-niyama embraces natural laws such as those of physics and chemistry. For example, when seeking an explanation for the occurrence of an earthquake we may be served better by the theory of plate tectonics than by the theory of Karma. The *bīja-niyama* governs the physical organic order, including the laws of biology. For example, if I catch a cold it would seem more sensible to explain this by supposing the presence of a virus rather than supposing 'moral' causes. The *mano-* or *citta-niyama* governs the laws of the mind and to some extent relates to psychology. The phenomenon of shock or post-traumatic stress may, for example, be best explained under this heading. The *karma-niyama* governs the sphere of volitional human conduct (including body, speech, and mind). In practice, it does not seem easy to separate the non-volitional and volitional mental spheres. The exact meaning of the *dharma-niyama* and what it governs is not clear. A traditional account links it to miraculous events in the Buddha's life, but it can also be thought of as the principle that underlies spiritual evolution.[40] Seen in this way, the *dharma-niyama* explains the process by which we can transcend our selfishness, hatred, and ignorance and achieve generosity, compassion, and understanding. In traditional terms, it explains how it is that we can break free from the determining influence of Karma and rebirth and so put a stop on the wheel of perpetual re-becoming. It underlies the dynamics of spiritual development.

A further way of thinking about the *dharma-niyama* is to see it as the 'undeserved' compassionate influence that someone may exert on our life. In other words, it is the impact of the saint on the world. The saint does not act towards others in accordance with their karma but deals compassionately with everyone, regardless of merit. The Bible, for instance, commands:

> Love your enemies, do good to those who hate you, bless those who curse you, pray for those who ill-treat you.[41]

A saint may choose to help – rather than avoid – an evil person precisely *because* they are evil and in need of redemption. Within Buddhism, this attitude is embodied mythically in the figure of Kṣitigarbha.[42] Out of compassion, Kṣitigarbha makes those beings who suffer the terrible outcome of their own karma his special concern. He is aware that, left to their own devices, they will simply compound their wretchedness by continuing to behave in harmful ways. So he intervenes in order to help them break the negative cycle and find a way out of their self-created hell. A more concrete example of this is a drug rehabilitation programme which, rather than treating addicts as criminals who should be punished, sees them as being in desperate need of help. Despite what they may have done, some compassionate people still want to help drug addicts because they understand that, without external support, they will never be able to help themselves. We don't always get what we 'deserve'; sometimes we get much more and sometimes much less. In this sense at least, the universe is not completely 'fair'.

The five-*niyama* analysis of experience shows that Karma is just one application of the general principle of dependent origination and, therefore, many circumstances and outcomes are likely to be governed by conditions only very indirectly related to Karma itself. But we should beware of seeing these different orders of conditionality as completely discrete. In reality, there are not five distinct orders of conditionality. This is only a map of what happens. Every experience comprises a vast network of conditions; our previous moral conduct will often have a bearing on our present experience, but in many situations non-moral factors may well exert a more decisive influence. The teaching of the five *niyamas* thus presents a more complex and subtle account of why things happen as they do than the crude view of Karma criticized above. We need also to remember that the actions of other people may be more decisive in any given situation than our own karmic stream; it may be their evil or their goodness that causes us to suffer or benefit, rather than our own.

In conversation in the Bamboo Grove at Rājagaha, one of the Buddha's closest disciples, Sāriputta, asks him about the origin of suffering. Is suffering created by oneself or by another? Is it created both by oneself and another? Is it fortuitous?[43] The Buddha replies that suffering arises in dependence upon conditions. He points out that without sense contact (physical or mental) no suffering is possible. Singling out this condition illustrates that a number of conditions must be present before the experience of suffering – or indeed joy – becomes possible; Karma is just one of them.

In conclusion, it does not seem appropriate to assume that people are suffering as a result of their previous karma. While this is one possibility, there are a number of other options, as illustrated by the five *niyamas*. Sangharakshita, my own teacher, has suggested a methodology for responding to adversity that avoids some of the possible dangers inherent in the 'all-is-Karma' view. We should, he says, exhaust all other possible explanations before thinking of attributing our suffering to Karma.

> Only after making every attempt to remove a certain condition, and finding that although other circumstances are favourable an unknown factor frustrates all our efforts, are we entitled to apply the method of residues and conclude that the condition is due to karma.[44]

4

WHAT IS A KARMA?

S ome people say that the principle of Karma can be summed up in the phrase 'actions have consequences', but it says a lot more than this. As the teaching of the five *niyamas* illustrates, Karma is not a general law of causation. It is not even a general law of action. It is a practical teaching that underpins Buddhist ethics. It accounts for how our deliberate behaviour leads not only to the transformation of our moral character – for better or worse – but our relationships with other people, and even the world that we live in. So what exactly makes an act a karma?

The Importance of Intention

Remember that in Brahmanism, a karma was a *ritual* act – its effectiveness depended on the proper execution of a specified ritual. Karmas had prescribed values, which generated a certain quantity of merit (or demerit) irrespective of the individual actor's state of mind. But the Buddha understood Karma in quite a different way. He saw that the *intention (cetanā)* or volition that motivates an action is what is most important.[45] Any overt physical or verbal behaviour is secondary (though not insignificant).[46] So the karmic value of an action cannot be known by observing just its surface form; it requires an understanding of the motivation that gave rise to it. This motivation is not always obvious, since two actions may seem superficially similar but be inspired by contrary motives. For example, let's say two people give me presents, even the same present. The first does so because he wants to suck up to me in order that he may later borrow my car whereas the second has noticed that I am a bit down and wants to cheer me up. The two actions will have different karmic values because they are driven by different intentions, so they will have different consequences (even if I am taken in by the bribery).

Intentions can broadly be classified into two kinds or modes: skilful (*kusala*) and unskilful (*akusala*). Skilful intentions are born from generosity, compassion, and understanding; unskilful intentions are rooted in craving, aversion, and spiritual ignorance, collectively known as the three unwholesome roots.[47] Skilful actions are said to lead to desirable consequences and unskilful actions to undesirable ones. Learning to discriminate between skilful and unskilful desires, and acting on the skilful, is the foundation of Buddhist ethics. In practice, though, our motives are usually mixed – some skilful, some unskilful – and this will have a bearing on the resulting consequences.

But what is an intention? It is a deliberately willed action carried out by a being capable of moral judgement. This means that only beings able to deliberate about their moral choices and consciously direct their behaviour can perform karmas. So Karma does not apply to animals, babies, or severely mentally impaired people (in so far as they are unable to make moral distinctions and reflective decisions). But willed action has to be understood here broadly.

There are many actions which we will, but of which we are not particularly conscious while they are happening. For instance, when we drive a car we are willing the gear changes, braking, acceleration, and so on, but our mind may be on 'automatic'. Despite not always being conscious of our willing from moment to moment, we are still making a choice – to drive the car – so we must bear responsibility for the consequences of this. How our actions will modify our own future, the world around us, and the responses of others will be influenced by the degree to which there is 'intentional weight' behind our conduct. While our habitual, semi-conscious behaviour probably makes up the bulk of our karmic activity, some singular acts may be decisive in determining our karmic future.

Sometimes people are coerced into doing things that they would not normally do, things they even believe are wrong. And yet, through fear, they still do them. Are these intentional acts? Rather than pursue a legal definition of intention, let's look at an example. As a result of the 'Great Escape' of Allied aircrew from Stalag Luft III in the Second World War, Hitler ordered the execution of fifty of the recaptured escapees. One German soldier was ordered to shoot two of these men, an act that went against his own conscience and the conventions of war, yet he went ahead and shot them anyway – perhaps out of fear of reprisals from the SS. After the event the soldier felt deep remorse for his action but was still arrested and hanged by the Allies.

Despite his moral misgivings, the soldier chose to obey a wicked order and so must bear responsibility for this. This is a tragic story and probably few of us are likely to face such difficult choices – perhaps we would all act in the same way in the same circumstances – but, importantly, where there is choice there is moral responsibility and so karma. The soldier felt remorse because he knew that he *had* had a choice; he had chosen to value his own life above that of the airmen. While we must surely sympathize with his situation, it is nevertheless choices of this kind that enable dictators to remain in power.

It is worth noticing that spiritual ignorance is classed as unskilful. This means that we could act from seemingly positive motives and still behave unskilfully. A well-known proverb declares that 'the road to hell is paved with good intentions' and this holds good in relation to karma. The fact that 'I meant well' will not absolve me from the consequences of my lack of forethought. It is our responsibility to think through the potential consequences of what we do. For Buddhism, ignorance is a disposition; lack of awareness is a bad habit rather than an inevitable – and therefore excusable – condition of our being. To perpetuate our state of ignorance rather than overcome it is volitional and therefore has karmic implications.

Crucially, in Buddhism 'action' includes acts not only of the body but also of speech and mind. So even the thoughts that we don't act upon have karmic weight – not least because they play a significant role in the way that we colour our experience. More profoundly, we become what we think. Once we have learned to behave in a reasonably civilized way, thoughts, rather than overt actions, are likely to become our most influential karmas. Somewhat paradoxically, an overt action discharged on the basis of a fairly weak volition may, in some cases, be of less karmic significance than a constantly cherished thought that does not find physical expression. For instance, let's say that I go to my housemate's room and borrow some of his books, forgetting that he likes to be asked. This is called, in Buddhism, taking the not-given. But the karmic effect of this act may be less decisive than my daily practice of *mettā*, or loving-kindness, through which I deliberately cultivate positive emotions towards him. For Buddhism, thoughts are acts and have their own consequences, not least because sooner or later they are likely to be expressed verbally or physically.

While a karma is fundamentally an intention or volition, overt behaviour is also very important. It is, for instance, quite different to think vaguely about taking my friend a bunch of flowers when I go to visit him than actually to do so. Both the fantasy and the overt action are no doubt skilful karmas, but the latter demands more commitment and determination and will have more significant consequences in all sorts of ways.

'Action' can also include 'omission', particularly when I have made a promise to act or have a duty to do so. All parents, for instance, have a duty to protect, feed, and clothe their children. If they do not fulfil their obligations and harm comes to their children, they must bear the moral responsibility (and may also be held legally accountable). But moral duties of this kind are not always clear-cut. How far does our duty to help the starving in the developing countries extend, for instance? If we didn't contribute to a famine appeal, would we be implicated in the consequent deaths of those who received no food? Looked at from this point of view, our duty to assist others becomes an impossible burden, as there are so many beings in need. But let's say that when we hear about the appeal on the news, we stifle our urge to give, at the very least we will be starving the impulse within us that seeks to reach out and respond to the suffering of others. This itself is a karmic consequence that will transform the kind of person we become. The more we ignore the positive ethical impulses that spark within us, the more we erode our moral sensibility.

Another way of talking about Karma is to say that it is about *choice*, but choice as understood in a broader sense than usual. Let me explain. A significant choice – and one that we were very much behind at the time – might lead us to embark on a series of actions. When we make the first choice we are, as it were, also choosing the possible consequences of that choice. Understanding this point is crucial in deepening our ethical sensitivity. If we reflect on it, our understanding of the gravity of the present moment may well intensify, because we will realize that what we are about to do may set in train a series of events that will have repurcussions far into the future. We usually think very little about the choices we make, but just a little imagination can enable us to realize how even quite casual decisions can significantly determine our destiny.

For example, some years ago, a young merchant banker called Nick Leeson, who worked for Barings Bank, decided to speculate on the stock market using bank funds. He thought he would make some money, replace the funds, and no one would be any the wiser. But he lost money. To win it back and cover up his deceit, he invested still more of Barings' funds, but he lost more money. He then began cooking the books in order to cover up his mistakes, lost more money, and eventually brought about the collapse of the bank. He was later arrested and imprisoned. At first he had no thought about bringing down the bank, or even defrauding it, but his first gamble led him into a series of further gambles which resulted in consequences that he neither foresaw nor welcomed. This nightmarish scenario of life spiralling out of control could happen to anyone.

So we make choices at different levels. While in principle we are completely free, in practice we can only exercise our freedom by committing ourselves to a particular course of action. By definition, we cannot then follow others, so any choice involves a narrowing of subsequent choices and this can leave us with an undesirable choice – one we would rather not make, but we are obliged to. Any major life decision is likely to bind us to other decisions that we hadn't foreseen and might not want to go along with. In making the first choice, we are choosing these too. Learning to imagine the consequences of our decisions can lead us to act in a more reflective, intelligent, and conscious way. This heightens our awareness of the gravity of the present moment; what we do *will* change the world, however imperceptibly. We will have to live with the consequences of our decisions.

Spiritually evolving individuals are not only more able to take responsibility for their choices but also, as they grow, recover *more* choice. How is this so? The relatively unaware person stumbles through life making decisions with huge implications, but often without recognizing that they have done so. Because they don't recognize they have made choices, they cannot review or change them, so they experience life as though it is directed by forces outside their control. As a result, they may end up blaming other people – usually an authority such as the government – because they are in a situation that they don't like and they feel unable to change it. But as soon as we discard the belief that we can determine our own lives, we disenfranchise ourselves, we become victims, and spiritual progress becomes a matter of accident rather than personal responsibility.

Choice in the karmic sense is not always obvious. Just because we fail to consider doing things differently, or are unaware that we could do so, doesn't mean that we have no choice. Lack of awareness is itself a choice, a habit, that we perpetuate moment by moment as long as we do nothing about it. In the course of our daily activities we don't consciously register many of our choices, which may partly explain why we sometimes feel resentful at some of their implications. The spiritual life involves becoming more and more aware of the choices we make, how we make those choices, moment by moment, and changing them in the light of our best values.

Not all the choices we make have the same karmic weight. Buddhist scholastic philosophy, for instance, identifies four grades of karma ranked according to their supposed order of priority. These are (1) weighty (*garuka*) karmas, (2) death-proximate (*maraṇāsanna*) karmas, (3) habitual (*āciṇṇa*) karmas, and (4) residual (*kaṭattā*) karmas.

A weighty karma is likely to have a decisive impact on the evolution of our being. Traditionally, unskilful weighty karmas comprise the five 'heinous crimes': killing one's mother, killing one's father, killing a saint (*arhant*), wounding a Buddha (apparently a Buddha cannot be killed), and causing schism in the spiritual community (*sangha*). Committing any of these acts leads to a rebirth in hell.[48] The only *skilful* weighty karma mentioned in the tradition is the entering of states of superconsciousness (*dhyāna*) through meditation. But we needn't stick rigidly to this schema. The general point is clear: if we do unskilful things, this will have a negative effect on our future lives, but acting skilfully will have a positive effect. Interpreting the notion of weighty karmas in a more contemporary way, we could say that a weighty karma is a decision or action that critically directs – or redirects – our lives. For instance, undergoing a religious conversion could be a weighty karma in this sense.

In the absence of a weighty karma, death-proximate karma comes into play. Most religions place importance on one's dying wishes and Buddhism is no exception. The intentions and aspirations that one exhales with one's last breath can have a powerful transforming effect, and – traditionally – improves one's chances of a good rebirth. Even if we don't believe in rebirth, what we dwell on at death is probably a reliable gauge as to the kind of life we have lived and the values we hold most dear.

The third grade of karma is 'habitual'. This is 'bread-and-butter karma': what we are doing most of the time. The precise effects of a single habitual karma may not be easy to see, but each time we act out a habit the more likely we are to act it out again. Slowly, over months and years, we sculpt our character just as a potter gradually moulds the clay.

The final grade of karma is 'residual', which accounts for anything not covered by the other three categories. It would, for example, cover ordinary, everyday karmas that were neither weighty nor committed habitually. For instance, in a moment of recklessness we might go shop-lifting, but if we only do it once it does not become a habit. Clearly this will have some sort of effect on our life but it might not be easy to determine what exactly the effect is; it might simply be that we would feel some remorse the following day and want to make amends.

So karmas are not all of the same kind – some are more influential and decisive than others. A weighty karma may, for instance, override the influence of a habitual karma, while a habitual karma may 'cancel out' a residual karma.

Two Important Assumptions

Karma rests upon two important assumptions about human character. The first assumption is that human character is not fixed, and so it may be modified. The second is that willed actions are the means by which character is modified. Looking at these claims will help to clarify how Karma works.

1. Human Character is Malleable

The common-sense view of human personality is that it is fairly static. This view is often associated with a belief in an eternal, unchanging soul, such as that of Christian doctrine. Many people, not only Christians, believe there is an essence to the person – there is something about each individual that is substantial and permanent. This belief seems to be borne out by our experience: people have recognizable personalities, behave in habitual ways, and don't usually change very much. But according to Buddhism this view is wrong: it arises from existential insecurity, a need to feel substantial, real, permanent. Without denying the obvious way in which people do have distinct personalities, Buddhism rejects the claim that there is anything fixed and unchanging in an absolute sense. If this were the case, the principle of dependent origination would be fatally flawed and spiritual evolution would be impossible. While recognizing the continuity of human personality, Buddhism says that this personality is malleable. There are no limits to the possibilities for individual transformation: a timid person may become confident, a Scrooge benevolent, an angry person tranquil, a clumsy person mindful. Like everything else, our personalities and character traits are dependent upon conditions and, should those conditions cease, they will change.

This malleability of character, and especially of one's moral relations with others, is beautifully illustrated in George Eliot's story, *Silas Marner*. Silas, a respected elder in a small religious sect, is falsely accused of theft. He is 'convicted' through the drawing of lots. Thus begins his first moral transformation. With his faith shattered, he leaves his home village to settle in Raveloe. Taking refuge in his work, and shunning fickle humanity, Silas starts to accumulate a hoard of gold. Embittered by his unfair treatment, he ceases to care for anyone or anything except his growing wealth. Day by day, he becomes more miserly, and more misanthropic.

Some time later, Dunstan, a wayward son of the local squire, steals Silas Marner's gold. Silas is again crushed by the way life has treated him, but the thief is not unmasked and Silas is plunged into poverty. Some months later, Silas finds a young girl who has wandered into his house. By following her tracks in the snow, he discovers her mother, who has tragically died. Silas interprets the girl, whom he names Eppie, as a blessing that has come to replace his gold. He learns to love her – and she him – and, in this way, his spirit is transformed; his hatred for humanity resolves. This is his second moral transformation.

Many years later, Silas and Eppie go to visit Silas's old home, which has been torn down to make way for a factory. This experience frees him from his cursed past and enables him to return home in peace. The miracle of Eppie has caused him to trust in life and to overcome his resentment of the injustices he has suffered. This story, initially tragic but ultimately uplifting, shows how our character can not only deteriorate but also rejuvenate during the course of our lives.

2. Volitional Actions Modify Character

Karma not only says that human character is malleable but that our character is modified by the volitional actions we carry out. Looking at a traditional Buddhist analysis of the human being will help explain this. Buddhist teaching divides the human being into five aspects (*skandhas*, literally 'heaps'): form, feeling, perception, volitional dispositions, and consciousness.[49] Rather than give a full account of these aspects, we will concentrate on just one of them: volitional dispositions (*saṃskāras*). What makes each individual recognizable and unique is the sum total of his or her volitional dispositions. Our volitional dispositions are our tendencies to act, speak, and think in a particular way. They are what determine our habits and thus what make us distinctive. They constitute those aspects of our character which others are constantly praising or complaining about. Depending on our particular moral make-up, some of these habits will be skilful, others unskilful. Owing to their relative continuity, we tend to think that these habits are enduring and unchanging, but this is a mistake that prevents us reforming them and realizing our potential.

Our 'essence', to the extent that this term means anything, is that we are a constantly changing bundle of habits. Every time we undertake a volitional act, a particular tendency is reinforced, and every time we resist the temptation of another course of action, we undermine the strength of the volition that would carry it out. In this way, we change from moment to moment. But in the short term that change is usually imperceptible; it becomes significant only after many years. Sudden, cataclysmic personal changes are rare, although not unknown.

Understanding the dynamic of personal change can help us to take on board the slow, painstaking, even laborious nature of personal transformation. We can't completely change ourselves overnight because our more deeply ingrained patterns of thinking, feeling, speaking, and behaving require consistent attention over a prolonged period if they are to be changed. There is no quick fix. At the same time, while progress may be slow and difficult, it *is* possible. It is because we have no fixed, unchanging self that we can become spiritually liberated.

5

THE FRUITS OF KARMA

A karma consists fundamentally in a choice, though this choice will not necessarily lead to overt action or speech. But if a choice is not acted out what kind of effect could it have? The consequences that arise from karmas are technically known as *vipākas* (effects) or *phalas* (fruits). So what kinds of effect do karmas bring about? What is the nature of karmic fruit? It is often said that we 'reap what we sow', as though a karma automatically led to a specific result. But just as a good harvest depends not only on sowing but also on many other factors (such as the weather), so karmas take effect in accordance with the general principle of conditionality.

We have already established that Karma is a principle of moral agency and not a general causal principle. It follows that only those consequences informed by the moral impetus behind an action are results of karma. Many of the consequences resulting from what we do are better explained by other factors. For instance, if I throw a ball from a window it falls to the ground not because I am good, bad, or indifferent; it falls because that is what bodies do. This particular fruit, or consequence, will not be significantly affected by my moral condition; whether I am good, bad, or indifferent the result will almost certainly be the same, because it is governed by the *utu-niyama*, the physical in-organic order, and not the *karma-niyama*.

According to Brahmanism, the fruits of karma ripen only from lifetime to lifetime and not within the current life. So in our next life we will reap the fruit of the karmic seeds we sow in this one and, at the same time, sow further karma for our subsequent life. This means we have no hope of changing the pattern of our present life, but must trust that we will experience the 'rewards' of our good karma in the life to come. There is a considerable leap of faith involved in adopting this point of view. Buddhism expanded the range of options as to when karmas could ripen to include four possibilities: (1) Karma that has consequences in this life, (2) Karma that has consequences in the next life, (3) Karma that has consequences in some future life, and (4) Karma that becomes exhausted before taking effect (see p.77).

The *Cūḷakammavibhaṅga Sutta*[50] describes how the relationship between karma and its consequences was understood in early Buddhism. It examines seven different actions and their opposites, and charts the consequences that follow from each in one's next life (see table opposite). It claims, for instance, that if we kill living beings, then, in our next life, we will be short-lived. It also claims that if we are of an angry disposition we will be reborn ugly. A direct correlation is made between karma and consequence in a 'punishment-to-fit-the-crime' sort of way. It is certainly all very neat. The kinds of consequences attributed to karma here are very diverse, embracing lifespan, physical health, appearance, social importance, economic situation, caste or class, and level of intelligence. Interestingly, apart from intelligence, none of the supposed consequences of one's karma relate to one's future character. To me this suggests a way in which Buddhist thinking about Karma was still deeply influenced by Brahmanical thinking. Not only is the psychological dimension of Karma not fully appreciated, but Karma is seen as the main (if not sole) explanation for the differences between people – why, for instance, some people suffer and others don't. In looking at the five *niyamas*, we have already seen that this is not always the case.

The relationship between kamma and vipāka according to the *Cūḷakammavibhaṅga Sutta* (Majjhima Nikāya 135)			
kamma		**vipāka**	
kusala or skilful	*akusala* or unskilful	*sugati* or happy consequence	*duggati* or unhappy consequence
not killing beings	killing beings (*paṇātipāta*)	long-lived (*dīghāyuka*)	short-lived (*appāyuka*)
not harming beings	harming beings (*viheṭhaka*)	healthy (*appābādha*)	sickly (*bavhābādha*)
not angry	angry (*kodhana*)	beautiful (*pāsādika*)	ugly (*dubbaṇṇa*)
not envious	envious (*issāmanaka*)	influential (*mahesakkha*)	impotent (*appesakkha*)
generous (*dātar*)	not generous	rich (*mahābhoga*)	poor (*appabhoga*)
reverential and humble	obdurate and haughty (*thaddha, atimānī*)	high-born (*uccākulīna*)	low-born (*nīcākulīna*)
asks about the skilful	doesn't ask about the skilful (*kusala*)	wise (*mahāpaññā*)	stupid (*duppaññā*)

There are many stories in the early Buddhist tradition that superficially teach a rather literal relationship between karma and *vipāka*. For instance, the *Udāna* ('Verses of Inspiration') re-cords the story of Suppabuddha, a leper, who stumbles upon the Buddha delivering a discourse while out begging for scraps of food.[51] He instantaneously gains transcendental insight, but is killed by a mad cow immediately afterwards. Later, the Buddha is approached by some of his followers who ask why it was that Suppabuddha became a leper. The Buddha's reported answer is that in a previous life Suppabuddha had insulted a saint (*arahant*) by calling him a leper and spitting in his face. For this evil deed he suffered in hell for many hundreds of thousands of years and, as a residual result, was reborn as a leper.

While the 'poetic justice' suggested here may have a certain emotional, even aesthetic appeal, such a symmetrical under-standing of the relationship between a particular karma and its experienced effect oversimplifies the complex and often messy nature of real events. We could see this model of Karma as a 'folk model' that worked in the sense that it discouraged people from acting unskilfully and spurred them to good deeds. Philo-sophically, though, it seems to ignore the different orders of con-ditionality. Such rather literal correlations between karmas and their effects may be better understood as illustrating the general truth that unskilful actions will have undesirable consequences and skilful actions will have desirable consequences, rather than being taken as exact descriptions of what actually happens.

Levels of Karmic Consequence

We have already noted that not all the consequences resulting from a morally informed action are *vipākas*. An action may have all sorts of consequences that have very little to do with the ethi-cal condition of the agent who performed them. More than this, a karma can have a range of possible consequences that may or may not come about depending upon whether other conditions are also present. Following this reasoning, we can identify 'direct' results of karmas and more 'indirect' ones.

The most direct results of a karma are mental. In other words, through performing karmas (which are ultimately intentions), we change our minds and, bit by bit, reform our character. To understand this more fully, we need to return to the concept of *saṃskāras* or volitional tendencies. Because there is no fixed soul, no essential person, only a jumble of habits and tendencies, we identify our 'self' with those dominant habits and tendencies. If we have a tendency to become angry, we think of ourselves as an angry person; if we tend to be very quiet, we may think of ourselves as a timid person. In this way, we define ourselves in terms of the particular character traits and habits we experience most strongly. We could even say that what we are is no more than a habit.

Well, not quite. Since Karma is essentially about choice, we always have the option of not going along with our habits, and taking a different turning at the crossroads. The chances are that our karmic momentum will lead us to reinforce our present

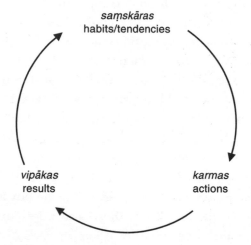

FIG. 2: THE CYCLE OF HABIT FORMATION

habits unless we consciously and deliberately work against them (fig. 2). This is why it can prove very difficult to change. The weight of our previous choices seems to push us in a particular direction and it might take a lot of effort to resist this. But this is the workplace of spiritual life: in recognizing our habitual tendencies, realizing it is possible to resist them, and in making new choices about who we want to be. If we make a new choice, the possibility of a new habit arises and, ultimately, the possibility of a new self. However enmeshed we are in a particular set of habits, however unskilful we have become, there is always the possibility of change. Thus Buddhism expresses a supremely optimistic vision of human nature; it never gives up on anyone, but recognizes that, even in the most evil of characters, there is always the potential for redemption.

Not only does our previous karma have implications for our character, it also has implications for the kind of world we live in, or at least the way we experience that world. For instance, someone who experiences a lot of fear sees the world as dangerous and threatening, whereas for someone who is very confident the world seems mild and compliant. Neither of these perspectives can be fully 'objective', but we tend to believe that our way of experiencing the world is the way the world really is. Fundamentally, we create our own world and don't realize how much our own prejudices, desires, and habits distort our experience of it; we see the world in terms of our selves. Learning to disentangle what is the given in experience and what is our evaluation is a subtle and complex process requiring ever-increasing levels of awareness, honesty, and perceptiveness.

But our actions also have ramifications beyond ourselves. They may have all sorts of consequences for the physical world and for other people too. While these also arise partly in dependence upon the initial intention, their precise outcome is not determined by it. For instance, if Green murders Blue the most

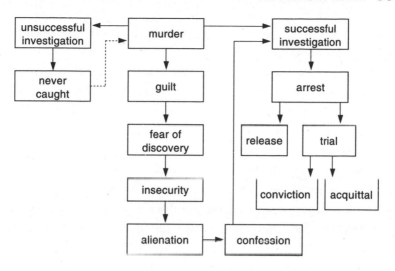

FIG. 3: A POSSIBLE KARMIC CHAIN (SIMPLIFIED)

direct outcome is likely to be a fear of being caught, and perhaps a sense of isolation from society, even a sense of guilt. After all, Green is now a murderer. Given that our society has laws against murder, a further outcome might be that he is arrested, tried, and convicted. Depending on where he lives, he might even be executed. But this will not necessarily happen, and even if it does it is not simply the result of Green's karma. It may be that the police lack expertise in following up clues, so they never discover the murderer. Perhaps the prosecution makes a mistake in its preparation and Green is acquitted. All sorts of conditions could come into play such that Green does not end up getting caught or convicted, but this is not necessarily because Green has performed good karmas in the past. The world is not as neat and tidy as that. Instead, there is a complex interaction of karmic streams and other non-karmic factors which collectively produce a unique scenario. The karmas of the police have an important bearing on the outcome, as do the karmas of the barristers and the jury. Someone might be falsely acquitted or even falsely convicted, and these eventualities might say nothing about their moral condition.

This process is shown in fig. 3. We can see that the chain of consequences can stop at a number of points and what keeps the chain intact may have more to do with the actions of others than it does with the primary agent. At the same time, without the initial act no chain would be formed. So in contemplating a particular course of action, the ethically responsible person must not only examine their present moral state but also consider the potential consequences of their conduct. This act of imagination can bring greater moral weight to our deliberations, otherwise we may find that our past actions return to haunt us. This is the theme of Thomas Hardy's tragic novel, *The Mayor of Casterbridge*. At the beginning of the story, Henchard, a poor journeyman labourer, sells his wife in order to make some money. This enables him to begin a new life and he eventually works his way up to become an important man – the mayor of Casterbridge. Everything seems to be going swimmingly until his wife reappears and his dark secret is disclosed. This leads ultimately to his downfall.

While it is true that consequences that no one could have foreseen sometimes result from our actions, it is usually the case that a little thought could enable us to predict the likely outcome of our actions. Crucially, we need to take responsibility for our contribution to any state of affairs.

Do We Always Get What We Deserve?

According to the *Dhammapada*,

> Not in the sky, nor in the midst of the sea, nor yet in the clefts of the mountains, nowhere in the world (in fact) is there any place to be found where, having entered, one can abide free from (the consequences of) one's evil deeds.[52]

But it seems that many people commit evil deeds and don't suffer as a result. How can Karma account for this? Another sutta, the *Mahākammavibhaṅga* ('Greater Discourse on Karma'),[53] goes some way towards providing an explanation. Here the Buddha identifies four kinds of person: (1) someone who acts evilly and is reborn in an unfavourable realm (even in hell), (2) someone who acts evilly and is reborn in a favourable realm (even in heaven), (3) someone who acts skilfully and is reborn in a favourable realm (even in heaven), and (4) someone who acts skilfully and is reborn in an unfavourable realm (even in hell).

We need not accept the principle of rebirth to understand the problem being tackled here. It could be rephrased along the following lines: (1) someone who acts evilly and seems to suffer later on, (2) someone who acts evilly who seems to have a good life later on, (3) someone who acts skilfully and who seems to have a good life later on, and (4) someone acts skilfully and who seems to suffer later on.

The question at issue here is how someone could act skilfully and yet suffer as a consequence (even being reborn in hell), and, conversely, how could someone act unskilfully and seem to benefit (even being reborn in heaven)? These outcomes seem to contradict the principle of Karma: the claim that actions give rise to commensurate consequences. Not so, says the Buddha. It would be a mistake to draw such a conclusion before looking further into the matter. The Buddha further points out that the evil-doer who goes to heaven must have acted skilfully in order to do so, but at some time in the future will reap the consequences of their evil conduct. Similarly, the person who acts skilfully but goes to hell must have acted evilly at some time in the past but will later reap the positive consequences of their good conduct.

This sutta is valuable because it demonstrates awareness of the apparent contradiction between what we sometimes see around us – and even experience – and the doctrine of Karma. People who act well sometimes suffer, whereas people who act badly sometimes don't. The relationship between karma and *vipāka* is not a simple, linear one; we might not be able to trace the precise connection between a given karma and its *vipāka*, unless the karma is weighty. Our current experience is informed by our past actions, but precisely how each of those actions shapes the present might be indiscernible because the *vipāka* resulting from each distinct karma will often be quite subtle. It is more like baking a cake: we combine all sorts of ingredients and cook them, but when we taste the finished product we don't experience the ingredients separately. In the same way, our life has a particular flavour determined by the ingredients (past karmas) we have put into it. For the purposes of exposition, we single out a particular action and its consequence, but we don't normally experience life like this. Rather than imagining a one-to-one correspondence between a particular karma and its *vipāka*, we can think instead of experiencing an overall karmic momentum that has been set in motion by a large cluster of actions.

But the defence of Karma attributed to the Buddha in the *Mahākammavibhaṅga Sutta* only fully works if we accept rebirth. Let's say someone acts badly throughout their life but does not seem to suffer as a consequence – they are not burned by a fire from heaven, they don't lose their relatives, they don't lose their wealth, nor are they persecuted in any way.[54] Without the prospect of rebirth in an undesirable realm (*duggati*), they seem to have 'got away with it'. There is nothing more repugnant to the conventionally moral person than to see this happen, and it can be quite undermining. Let's say I act morally all my life yet I experience all sorts of suffering, calamity, and difficulty while my evil neighbour seems to live an easy existence. There seems to be something inherently unjust about this. It seems unnatural. In such circumstances, why should I bother being ethical? If I can comfort myself with the prospect that he will roast in hell as a consequence of his conduct and that I will soon be in heaven, I can perhaps be persuaded to put up with the present injustice. But if we don't accept rebirth – and many Westerners will not – does this sort of scenario undermine the rationale for living ethically?

It need not. The way of thinking just described is rather narrow in that it looks for specific rewards for good conduct and punishments for bad. This is to miss the point. It is a cliché that 'virtue is its own reward' but it is nevertheless still true. We should not see our ethical conduct as a contract or an investment, but aim to forget ourselves, at least for a moment, in going beyond our own needs and desires in order to respond to somebody else. This self-forgetting can be a tremendous relief from self-preoccupation. It can be liberating.

Through our morally positive conduct, we can not only benefit other people but also transform ourselves. The moment-by-moment decisions that we make slowly mould our character. If we always act from our best motives we will develop a clear conscience, perhaps one of the greatest boons one could hope for. The sense of guilt, of wrongdoing, that hangs over many people's lives crushes the spirit and can even lead to madness. Just as water corrodes iron, so our evil actions corrode our spirit and eventually destroy it.[55] Accordingly, simply because an evildoer is not punished in some tangible way does not mean that person does not suffer as a result of his or her actions.

But there do seem to be some contrary individuals who don't appear to suffer – even psychologically – as a result of their evil conduct. Don't they undermine the notion of Karma? Here I want to introduce an unusual way of seeing what suffering is. It may be true that such people don't consciously experience suffering – they don't feel remorse or guilt for what they have done and seem to lead an enjoyable life. However, someone who is insensitive to their own evil is, to that extent, inhuman. They are cut off from the world of ordinary human beings and from their spiritual potential. They are condemned to an impoverished existence in which they are no longer able to feel, because to feel deeply would also mean recognizing their own evil. This impoverishment is itself a form of suffering.

Let me use an analogy. In recent years, there has been a move within the Christian church to redefine Hell as the absence of God. Transposing this way of thinking, we could say that at least one form of suffering is being cut off from feeling deeply for other human beings and from one's spiritual possibilities. In other words, limitation is itself a form of suffering even though it may not be consciously experienced as such.

We may be able to accept that others do not always reward virtue, we may even be able to accept that evil is not always punished, but what about when virtue seems to get punished? This would seem the last straw for the notion of Karma. It is a perverse fact that many ethical people, even saints, suffer terribly at the hands of others. Yet, if Karma is true, this should not be so. Of course, we can always speculate that they are only suffering as a consequence of their evil conduct in a previous life, but this presupposes a belief in rebirth which for many people is counter-intuitive. So is it possible to hold to a belief in Karma and accept the persecution of saints?

I think it is. A fact that the basic account of Karma usually leaves out is that we live in a world of other people who themselves make choices, act out habits, and follow through their karmic momentum in various ways. They impinge on our lives. We do not live in a world where we simply act and then experience the consequences of that action. Instead, our world is a swirling dance of karmic streams interacting with each other; other people influence our lives and we influence theirs. Since we do not live in a cocoon protected from the effects of others' behaviour, unwarranted suffering becomes possible. The fact that we suffer at the hands of an evil person need not necessarily mean that we acted evilly in a previous life – or even in this one – it is just one of the hazards of living in a world in which there are evil people. It may even be that an evil person wants to hurt us precisely *because* of our moral integrity. This may be hard to accept. We generally need some explanation, even justification, for why we are suffering, and the possibility that it is somewhat arbitrary is cold comfort. But there are some events that seem hard to explain in any other way, such as natural disasters or the atrocities of psychopathic killers.

Having said this, we usually contribute to the situation so we need to take responsibility for this. For instance, the journalist Brian Keenan was kidnapped in Lebanon and held hostage for several years in appalling conditions.[56] He did not necessarily 'deserve' that experience of suffering, it need not have been a punishment for his previous evil conduct, but he did choose to be in Lebanon at a time when he knew that Westerners were regularly kidnapped. So Keenan played a role, he was one of the conditions that gave rise to his capture, but his karma did not make it happen. The unscrupulous terrorists who kidnapped him played their part too.

The way in which our karmic stream is intertwined with others is brilliantly illustrated in J.B. Priestley's play *An Inspector Calls*.[57] An Inspector Goole turns up unexpectedly at a family dinner party and announces that a young pregnant woman, Eva Smith, has just died in hospital after drinking disinfectant. Rather drunk and dismissive, the family can't see what all this has to do with them. By a sequence of moves, Goole shows how each member of the family has played his or her part in leading Eva to the point of suicide. Birling, the father, her one-time employer, sacked her for asking for a pay rise. Sheila, his daughter, then had Eva dismissed from her post at a draper's for apparently laughing at a dress that Sheila had tried on. Gerald,

Sheila's fiancé, then took Eva as his mistress and eventually deserted her. Then Birling's son, Eric, after throwing himself at Eva one night while drunk, got her pregnant and then abandoned her. Finally, Birling's wife Sybil refused to offer help when Eva asked her charitable organization for assistance.

The whole family is implicated in the tragedy. One of the questions the play invites is: who is responsible? The family members are divided between those who see the implications of their own conduct and experience a moral awakening (Sheila, Eric, and initially Gerald) and those who refuse to accept any moral responsibility (Birling, his wife, and later Gerald). It's clear that the young woman chose to take her own life, yet it is also clear that the conduct of the Birling family was a significant factor in leading her to this point. Sheila and Eric see deeply into the situation and become morally transformed by their awareness. They are able to understand how their conduct formed important links in a chain that resulted in a terrible tragedy. The others seek to evade any responsibility. Goole concludes his interrogation in the following way:

> But just remember this. One Eva Smith has gone – but there are millions and millions and millions of Eva Smiths and John Smiths still left with us, with their lives, their hopes and fears, their suffering, and chance of happiness, all intertwined with our lives, with what we think and say and do. We don't live alone. We are members of one body. We are responsible for each other.[58]

After Goole leaves, doubts are raised as to whether he was a real police inspector. Birling phones the police and discovers there is no such person. Along with Mrs Birling and Gerald, Mr Birling concludes that the whole thing was a hoax: there was no suicide, and the hospital confirms this. They begin to treat the whole affair as a magnificent joke. But Sheila can't.

> But you're forgetting one thing I still can't forget. Everything we said had happened really had happened. If it didn't end tragically, then that's lucky for us. But it might have done.[59]

The play ends with Mr Birling receiving a telephone call from the police. He is told that a young woman has died on her way to hospital after swallowing disinfectant....

Even if the outcome had not really been suicide, the fact remains that each member of the family had acted badly and the 'fictional' suicide was a means by which they could begin to take moral responsibility for their actions. This is a thought experiment that we could make use of when considering our own ethical challenges. By forecasting the potential consequences of whatever we propose to do, we will be better able to make the most creative decision. If we act badly, this does not necessarily mean we are responsible for everything that results, but we should at least be aware that we contributed a necessary link in a chain of events that could lead to a tragedy like the one in Priestley's play. This is rather sobering.

6

BENDING THE 'IRON LAW'

Karma is sometimes described as a principle of retribution, an impersonal cosmic judge who impartially punishes the wicked and rewards the righteous. If we act evilly, we will inevitably suffer; if we act well, we will thrive. Not only this but 'the punishment fits the crime'; if we steal from others then we will be burgled, and so on. We have already seen that this can be far from true and the consequences arising from our karmas depend on a number of factors, some of which have little or nothing to do with our ethical condition.

Any particular karma might have a whole range of results and very few of these are certain. Like everything else in the universe, the consequences of our actions depend on conditions; without the conditions that give rise to the consequences, those consequences won't come about. While it might seem natural justice that suffering should follow from evil conduct, it doesn't always do so. So what other factors might influence the operation of the 'iron law' of Karma, and can it be broken or even transcended?

Karmic Fruit is Conditioned by our Overall Ethical Condition

That Karma is an organic – as opposed to mechanical – principle is well illustrated in a sutta called the *Lonaphala* or 'Salt Crystal'.[60] This text proposes that our *vipākas* depend, at least in part, on our overall ethical condition, so much so that two people might commit the same act but experience different consequences. 'Imagine,' says the Buddha, 'that someone who neglects their spiritual development, who is unaware and careless, commits a trifling unskilful act. Well, that unskilful act may take them to hell after death. Now imagine a second person who takes care of their spiritual life, who is vigilant and insightful, a great soul (*mahatta*), but who commits a similar trifling unskilful act. That act may lead to consequences to be experienced in this life but which will be completely expiated by the time of rebirth.' How can this be?

The Buddha explains by use of an analogy. 'Suppose,' he says, 'a man dropped a crystal of salt into a little cup of water. Would the water become salty and undrinkable?' 'Yes,' his followers reply, 'of course it would.' 'But suppose then,' the Buddha continues, 'a man dropped a crystal of salt into the River Ganges, would it thereby become salty and undrinkable?' 'Surely not, Lord,' his followers reply. 'In just the same way,' the Buddha concludes, 'the minor wrongdoing of a worldling may take him to hell, whereas the minor wrongdoing of a spiritual person may be fully expiated in this very life.'

Just as light appears in different hues when seen through coloured filters, so the precise *vipākas* we experience are mediated through our overall ethical condition. In this sense, there is a *subjective* aspect as to how *vipākas* take effect. Through greater ethical sensitivity the spiritual practitioner is able to change for the better, an opportunity the less developed person does not have. Owing to more refined awareness, the spiritual person can recognize their own unskilfulness and therefore be in a position to address and transform it. Worldlings (*puthujjanas*), on the other hand, do not see their unskilfulness as such. This means that the fruits they reap are likely to have a greater conditioning influence on them, since they are unaware how their behaviour is distorting their character. They are therefore more likely to reinforce that unskilful behaviour rather than correct it.

Conscience and Vipāka

Ironically, a person with a tender conscience might seem to suffer more (through remorse) as a result of some slight unskilful behaviour than a person with little conscience who acts in a grossly unskilful way. While traditional Buddhism would say that the evil person will suffer in a future life, such solace presupposes a belief in rebirth.

It may be possible then that our suffering will *increase* as we develop spiritually. This is because, through ethical training, we develop our *conscience*. Conscience is a way of talking about our capacity to respond to events ethically and to make moral judgements. In traditional Buddhist terms, this capacity comprises *hiri* (personal shame) and *ottappa* (moral sensitivity to the wise). These two principles, known collectively as the 'bright protectors', enable us to discriminate between good and bad. *Hiri* could be described as our personal conscience; if we are about to act in a way that goes against our basic ethical values then *hiri* will come in and say 'Don't do that! It goes against what you stand for.' If, for some reason, *hiri* doesn't manage to prevent us acting on an unethical impulse, it will often arise later as a feeling of remorse, a recognition that we have morally let ourselves down. We may even burn with shame for what we have done.

Ottappa is more like our social conscience, particularly in relation to someone who embodies virtue. *Ottappa* arises when we imagine what a virtuous friend or teacher would think about our

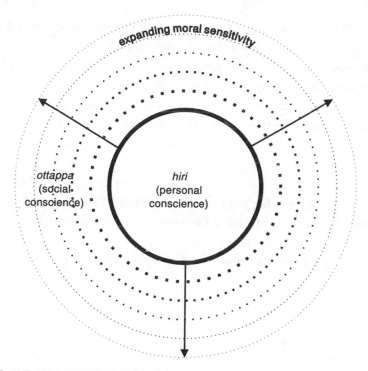

FIG. 4: THE EXPANDING CONSCIENCE

behaviour. By doing this, we introduce their higher ethical perspective into our decision-making process, thus expanding our
moral awareness. *Ottappa* thus backs up *hiri*; if *hiri* doesn't stop
us then *ottappa* might (fig. 4). *Ottappa* may thus be likened to a
guardian angel who sits on our shoulder and, on seeing that we
are contemplating an act that will lead to harm, intervenes.
Importantly, though, *ottappa* does not speak up automatically
since it is, ultimately, the creation of our own mind. We need to
make an imaginative leap if we are to make use of it and this
requires a certain degree of awareness. We need to be aware
enough to imagine what our ethical mentor might say about our
proposed course of action, and we need to be morally sensitive

to it. We may even need to hear them in our head and sense the disappointment they will feel if we go ahead.

As our experience of *hiri* intensifies, we become more ethically sensitive, expanding our awareness to see our moral failings more fully. We will begin to experience *more* shame and remorse because we become more sensitive to our wrongdoing. Experiencing *hiri* and *ottappa* more keenly is painful. Paradoxically, the ethically sensitive person might seem to suffer more than the ethically bankrupt one, but *hiri* and *ottappa* are supposed to be skilful emotions. Isn't this wrong-headed? One way to make sense of this uncomfortable situation is to think of human experience in terms of a 'band of awareness' (fig. 5). An undeveloped person has a fairly narrow band of awareness: they don't have

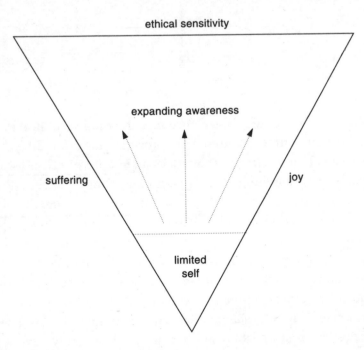

FIG. 5: THE EXPANDING BAND OF AWARENESS

much capacity to feel suffering, remorse, or moral responsibility, but neither do they feel much joy, generosity, or compassion. They lack sufficient imagination and awareness to understand the implications of their actions. Without this they do not feel remorse, so they do not suffer mentally as a result of their evil conduct (though this does not mean that their unskilful conduct has no impact upon them).

The ethically sensitive person, however, is able to empathize with people who suffer as a result of their unskilful deeds, and this leads them to experience remorse. Suffering is an imaginative act, which means that our capacity to suffer – and to feel the suffering of others – expands as our imagination develops. This might sound depressing, but the flip side is that our capacity to experience joy, pleasure, and significance expands proportionately as we learn to live in a larger emotional world, one in which we feel more connected to other human beings. Our 'reward' for skilful conduct is not necessarily happiness or pleasure but a 'greater soul'. As our capacity to imagine grows, our perspective on our own lives expands, allowing us to direct it consciously rather than being blown around by circumstance.

The unskilful person can develop morally too. When they do, the implications of their unskilful actions will become clearer to them. They may begin to feel remorse, even feel a need to confess and apologize, and so begin to grow beyond their previous evil. This can be a painful process. Even if we don't get 'punished' by the world, our own conscience may nag away at us as a result of our evil conduct. In order to blot out our scruples, we are in many cases forced to deliberately narrow our awareness – to ignore parts of our experience – because to embrace the whole would be to embrace our evil too. This means that while we continue to avoid responsibility for our unskilful conduct, we live in a half-world in which we are not really alive, not really aware, not fully ourselves. It is also true that if we have committed unskilful actions the burden of our dark secret can be very heavy, cutting us off from other human beings; we know that if they knew what we have done they would feel differently towards us, perhaps even avoid us. This leads to great insecurity; we don't want anyone to find out in case it destroys the life we are building up.

The case of Donald Crowhurst, who in 1968–9 took part in a single-handed yacht race, illustrates this point.[61] Owing to technical difficulties, he fell behind and began to keep a false log, which showed him to be performing far better than he actually was. He began to see a way of cheating in the race that would enable him to finish in a respectable position. For a while all went well. He had few qualms about his dishonesty until he realized that he was actually going to win the race. Shortly before arriving at the finish line, Crowhurst apparently threw himself overboard. It seems that he could neither face following through the logical consequence of his deception nor admit it.

Some people may never develop more than a rudimentary awareness of their moral condition and not suffer awakening to their own evil. They are in a state of ethical and even existential anaesthesia. Having little imagination, they may not suffer much at all, but they are not thereby free from karma and *vipāka*. They *are* the fruit of their past action; their previous conduct has moulded their character, their habits, their world. Their conduct will also have had an effect on other people, and this will have influenced the way others behaved towards them. While there may appear to be some benefits to remaining unaware, there is a heavy price to pay: we are forced to forgo an understanding of our own character, of how we came to be as we are, and of the possibility of changing it. Self-awareness can be both a blessing and a curse, a blessing because it creates the possibility of self-transformation, and a curse because we can no longer ignore the call to reform our lives.

Transference of Merit

A further question that has been important for Buddhism is this: can the actions of *others* modify our *karma-vipāka*? This question invites us to look at the doctrine of transference of merit, about which Buddhist tradition seems to be inconsistent. According to the *Pacchābhūmaka Sutta*,[62] a village headman approaches the Buddha and tells him that the Brahmans of the western lands claim to be able to take the spirit of a dead person, lift it out, instruct it, and send it to heaven. 'But,' continues the headman, 'I know that you, O Blessed One, can arrange things so that the whole world, after death, will reappear in a happy place, even in heaven.'

The Buddha responds with an analogy. 'Suppose,' he says, 'a man threw a great boulder into a deep lake and a large crowd of people gathered round the lake to pray, circumambulate, and cry out, "Rise up, O boulder! Rise up and come floating to the shore!" As a result of these prayers and entreaties, would the boulder rise up and float to the shore?'

'No,' the headman replies, 'naturally it wouldn't.' In the same way, the Buddha goes on to say, a man cannot be absolved from the consequences of his unskilful conduct as a result of the prayers and entreaties of others.

This sutta amounts to a light-hearted rejection of the orthodox Brahmanical belief that a son could, through the performance of appropriate rituals, intercede on his father's behalf to upgrade his destiny after death. Here the Buddha is suggesting that the actions of others cannot influence our lot beyond the grave and therefore cannot absolve us from the consequences of our actions. For this to happen would be a violation of a natural law – such as the law that heavy bodies fall.

But elsewhere Buddhist doctrine and practice is not always consistent with this view. The doctrine of 'transference of merit' supposes that it is possible to transfer the 'merit' (*puñña*, that is to say, positive *vipāka*) to a departed relative. For instance, it is common practice within Sri Lankan Buddhism to ritually offer food to the local monks after the death of a relative and then to 'transfer' the merit gained to the deceased.[63] Other kinds of offerings, such as the presentation of new robes to a monk, are also believed to add to one's stock of merit. Some Buddhist schools have believed that the amount of merit one accrues as a result of a donation depends, at least in part, on the ethical purity of the recipient. Some have also believed that each time a gift is used the donor gains more merit.[64] In this way, merit came to be seen as a kind of spiritual commodity independent of the individual's character, and its acquisition to depend, at least in part on factors outside their control. It then became important to make sure that those to whom one gave were as ethically pure as possible, as this would bestow the most merit. Since merit had become a spiritual commodity, it could be transferred or exchanged like money or goods and, consequently, could be used to 'save' another, an outcome completely at odds with the main thrust of early Buddhism.[65]

How have these somewhat bizarre beliefs and associated practices come about? To understand this we need to return to pre-Buddhist sources. In the Vedic tradition, it was believed that a departed spirit needed help from 'this side' either to gain a future rebirth or to attain the heavenly state. This was accomplished by the correct performance of prescribed rites. These rites usually involved some sort of food offering, the merit of which was then 'transferred' to the deceased. Within Buddhism, rather than make an offering to the gods, an offering is presented to the monks, and this earns merit which may then be transferred. The Vedic assumption that merit transfers are to be conducted mainly between family members also seems to have been adopted by Buddhism.

But transference of merit can also be understood in a much more ordinary, organic way than the magical view of the Vedic tradition. Many of our actions have implications for others. Our skilful actions can have a transformative, even revolutionary, impact on the lives of other people which may enable them to discard limiting beliefs and habits and embrace a more creative outlook. But the opposite is also true: our unskilful actions can undermine others, preventing them from developing positively, and encouraging them to indulge bad habits – or even to develop worse ones. When understood in this way, not only can we transfer our merit but we can also transfer our demerit (our evil) to others. The influence we exert upon others demonstrates that we do not live in discrete, insulated karmic bubbles; our moral behaviour can significantly alter the course of people's lives for better or worse. This is at the same time exhilarating and frightening; we really can help others to become free, but we can also help to imprison them. Learning to recognize the influence we have on others and using that influence wisely and compassionately is an essential aspect of spiritual growth. While we cannot save or damn another person, we can certainly help them save or damn themselves.

'Has-Been' Karma

Not only are our *vipākas* contingent on a whole range of factors, but some karmas may not fructify at all. How can this be? There is a notion found in Buddhist scholastic philosophy known as *ahosi* karma or 'has-been' karma. Since karmas require certain conditions in order to ripen, if those conditions do not appear it is possible that some karmas will never fructify. One of the ways this works is through counteractive behaviour. For instance, we might do something quite unskilful but, before experiencing any negative results, we act very skilfully to purify ourselves and, in this way, 'cancel out' the negative karma. Through a determined effort to develop the skilful, we can circumvent the negative *vipākas* that we would otherwise have experienced.

But karmic potential may even exhaust itself without the intervention of especially skilful conduct. While karma is sometimes presented as some sort of intangible thing that hangs around us waiting for the opportunity to reveal itself, the 'energy' of any karma is limited and if there is no immediate opportunity for its expression it may just 'fizzle out'.

I will illustrate this with a personal example. I first began smoking when I was about ten years old and carried on, more or less, until I was nineteen. Over this time I built up quite a strong habit, and smoking came to be closely bound up with my sense of personal identity. But then I moved into a community in which nobody smoked. I decided I wanted to give up smoking and, despite my long-term habit, did so almost immediately. I didn't need to make much effort to give up because the conditions that normally encouraged me to smoke were no longer present. Although I had quite a developed karmic propensity to smoke, this was dependent on certain conditions such as being around others who also smoked, or going to the pub. When I withdrew from these conditions I no longer experienced the strength of the habit and it very quickly withered. What was especially interesting was that I didn't even feel the desire to smoke: the habit dissolved completely. This sort of example reveals an important principle of self-transformation: our current habits are supported by conditions, so if we want to change we will often need to change our conditions in order to successfully break our habits. In new circumstances, it can sometimes be relatively easy to change oneself.

The Phenomenon of Conversion

Sometimes an event occurs in someone's life that constitutes a radical break with everything that has gone before. Nothing about their past conduct can account for the instant transformation that takes place. Such experiences can be described as conversions. Perhaps the most famous conversion is that of Saul, as recorded in the New Testament.[66] Himself a Jew, Saul's ultra-orthodox views led him to persecute the first followers of Jesus for flouting prevailing religious conventions. *Acts* records how he set out for Damascus planning to arrest some of them and bring them to Jerusalem for punishment. As Saul approaches Damascus, 'a light from heaven' flashes around him and he falls into a swoon. He hears a voice crying to him, 'Saul, Saul, why do you persecute me?'[67] It is the voice of Jesus, who orders Saul to continue to Damascus where he will be given further instructions. For three days Saul remains blind, but then a man called Ananias comes to him, blesses him, and his sight is restored. Almost immediately, the persecuting Saul turns into the fervent convert Paul (as he then calls himself), and goes on to establish what we now call Christianity. This transformation is miraculous. Little wonder, then, that the author of *Acts* saw it in terms of divine intervention. But transformations like Saul's are not uncommon, especially in religious literature.

There are similar examples in the Buddhist tradition. One of the best-known stories of miraculous conversion is that of Aṅgulimāla, a serial killer who chopped off the fingers of his victims and wore them in a gruesome necklace.[68] One day, the Buddha crossed his path. At first, Aṅgulimāla thinks he has trapped another victim, but he soon realizes he is dealing with no ordinary being. The Buddha inspires in him a profound spiritual transformation that leads him to renounce his evil ways and commit himself to spiritual practice within the Buddha's community. Shortly after his conversion, while begging in the local town, Aṅgulimāla comes across a woman giving birth to a deformed child. With his newly discovered sensitivity and compassion, he is deeply moved by this encounter. 'O how beings suffer!' he cries out. Later he meets up with the Buddha and tells him about the sad scene he has witnessed. 'In that case,' the Buddha responds, 'go back into Sāvatthi and say this to the poor woman: "I have never intentionally deprived a living being of life. By this truth, may you and your child be well."' Aṅgulimāla is dumbfounded. 'How can I go to her and say that, when I have killed so many people?' he says, 'It would be a lie.' 'Very well,' the Buddha replies, 'go to the young woman and say this: "Since I have become a follower of the Buddha, I have never intentionally taken life. By this truth may you and your child be well."' Aṅgulimāla does as the Buddha suggests and the woman and her child became well.

Regardless of whether all the details of this story are to be believed, it illustrates the principle that some transformations represent a complete break with the past through which the individual no longer experiences the influence, the 'habit-energy', of their previous conduct. In his 'new incarnation' as a Buddhist saint, Aṅgulimāla has not harmed anyone – he has been reborn. The end of this particular story is also interesting. When he next enters Sāvatthi, Aṅgulimāla suffers abuse from the townspeople and is pelted with stones. He returns to the Buddha, bruised and bleeding, his begging-bowl broken, his robe in tatters. According to the sutta, this suffering is punishment (*vipāka*) for Aṅgulimāla's previous evil, but I draw from it a different conclusion. Even though Aṅgulimāla has changed, the townspeople have not; they still see him as the evil serial killer, they have not forgiven him, and their instinctive urge for retribution remains. This is instructive. We may undergo a profound transformation that brings about a radical improvement in character and behaviour, but those around us may still treat us -

according to our past actions. So even though we might no longer 'deserve' punishment we might still get it. We might just have to bear this and accept that it takes time for others to catch up.

How can the kind of profound changes we have looked at best be explained? A Christian explanation might invoke the 'will of God', whereas a Buddhist might refer to the *dharma-niyama*. This spiritual order of conditionality can lead to positive events that cannot be understood using the notion of Karma alone. It is the bursting into flame of the spiritual spark that glimmers in everyone. The aim of Buddhist practice is not simply to perform good karmas – this is conventional 'goodness' only – but to *transcend* the operation of Karma and *vipāka*. The saint (*arhant*) whose mind is governed solely by the *dharma-niyama*, and so creates no more karma, exemplifies this transcendence. But what does it mean to transcend Karma? In everyday terms, it means undergoing permanent change, for instance, stopping a habit or addiction not just through discipline but because one no longer feels the need of the habit. It is a bit like when children grow away from their toys – there is no need to stop them playing with their toys, they are just not interested any more. This kind of 'growing out of' can be seen as analogous to breaking free of Karma, and it is the goal to which Buddhist life is directed.

The film *The Truman Show* offers a wonderful illustration of this kind of change.[69] Truman (played by Jim Carrey) lives in a cosy middle-American town. He has never travelled, never done anything unusual. He lives very much in his box. Unknown to him, he actually *does* live in a box because his entire life is a reality television show in which he is the star and everyone he knows is an actor. His life is fixed within a narrow range of possibilities determined by the show's director. Throughout his life Truman finds clues that things are not quite as they seem, but he fails to act on them. Finally, frustrated by the limitations he experiences, he determines to break out. He reaches the edge of his studio world and walks out through the sky into a new world, the dimensions and possibilities of which he could only have imagined. His discovery that he had been living in an artificially constructed world propels him into an expanded understanding of himself and his life, an understanding from which he cannot go back.

7

THE UNDISCOVERED
COUNTRY

Who would fardels bear,
To grunt and sweat under a weary life,
But that the dread of something after death,
The undiscovered country from whose bourn
No traveller returns, puzzles the will,
And makes us rather bear those ills we have
Than fly to others that we know not of?[70]

Death is a mystery; we just don't know what happens afterwards. We speculate, we fear, but in the end we don't
know. Since the unknown is often frightening, it is not surprising that many – if not all – of us seek some image or idea to help
us anticipate what we might confront when we finally shuffle
off this mortal coil. This is no doubt one of the reasons we turn to
a religion, because most of them offer a vision of what awaits us
when we die. Buddhism is no exception. It has always held to a
notion of rebirth or re-becoming, a belief that we are imprisoned
in a relentless cycle of birth and death (saṃsāra) until we achieve
liberation through spiritual awakening. Consequently, the early
Buddhist ideal was presented in terms of breaking free of the
wheel of life, death, and rebirth. While for the early Buddhist,

rebirth was a painful reality to be overcome, ironically, to many contemporary Westerners it seems a desirable option.[71]

There is little in the early Buddhist scriptures by way of argument in favour of rebirth.[72] In texts that aim to counter competing views that denied rebirth – 'wrong views' – the Buddha's experience is given as the 'proof' of its reality. But the Buddha and his early followers participated in a culture in which rebirth was widely, even if not universally, accepted; it was part of the frame of reference within which cultural life took place and spiritual liberation was pursued. If we have a quite different pattern of cultural assumptions, as many Western people do, how are we to approach the doctrine of rebirth? Is it something we should expect to have faith in, even if we have no experience of it? Is it just a primitive idea which we have outgrown? Is it to be taken literally? Or is it some kind of metaphor? Is it important to believe in rebirth if we are to engage with an effective spiritual life?

The Absence of 'Self'

The most important development within the Buddhist approach to rebirth was the assertion of *anātman* or 'no fixed self'. As a concept, this stood in opposition to other notions of the self that existed at the time. One of these asserted the existence of an *ātman* – an unchanging self that persisted through all our experiences. The Buddha denied this. However, *anātman* is not so much a philosophical truth as a spiritual realization, and we realize this truth through meditative exercises rather than intellectual reflection. Realizing *anātman* is to experience limitlessness, awakening to our unbounded nature. It is an experience of joy and freedom.

One of the main methods the Buddha used to trigger the realization of 'not-self' in others was meditation on the five *skandhas*

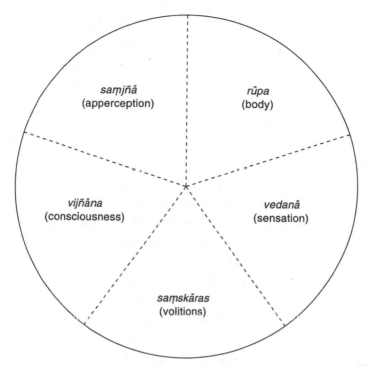

FIG. 6: THE SKANDHAS

or heaps (see fig. 6). The *skandhas* divide the human being into five aspects: consciousness, sensation, perception, volitions, and body. In meditation, we direct attention to each of these aspects of our experience and investigate whether that aspect is the self. Is the body my self? My sensations? My volitions? My perceptions? My experience of consciousness? In time, we come to realize that not one of the *skandhas* is stable and unchanging; they are all in flux. So where is the self? According to the Buddha, it is nowhere. 'Self' is a label we impose on our constantly changing experience; it has no reality. But this does not mean that we are nothing, and that our experience of being alive and being 'ourselves' is a delusion, only that our notion that we have a fixed identity that persists is a mistake. Recognizing this mistake

opens up new possibilities for personal transformation, allowing us to let go of limiting patterns of belief and behaviour, and
to develop new, more creative ways of experiencing the world.

If There is No Self, What is Reborn?

One of the knottiest questions the Buddhist approach to rebirth
throws up is this: if there is no fixed unchanging self, then what
is reborn? This question is not easily answered. It is important,
though, to understand that lack of a fixed self does not mean
lack of continuity. There is a good deal of stability within our
experience over the course of our lifetime, but while most
people maintain a more or less similar personality for their
whole lives and possess a fairly stable core of habits and beliefs,
stability and continuity do not entail unchanging identity.

The question of what is reborn and how the rebirth process
works has been one for which Buddhists down the ages have
struggled to find a convincing model. Possibly it is a difficulty
that is not really resolvable using concepts. In a post-canonical
Pali work known as *The Questions of King Milinda*, the king asks a
Buddhist monk called Nāgasena a number of questions about
the nature of the self and rebirth. This work records the kinds of
questions that arise in response to the Buddhist teachings, many
of which are still relevant today. First, Milinda asks whether the
person who is reborn is the same as or different from the person
who has died. Nāgasena replies that he is neither, which
suggests there can be no adequate concepts for expressing the
true nature of the relationship between the two. When pressed,
Nāgasena gives an illustration.

> In the case of a pot of milk which turns first to curds, then to
> butter, then to ghee; it would not be right to say that the
> ghee, butter and curds were the same as the milk but they

have come from that so neither would it be right to say that they are something else.[73]

Later Milinda asks Nāgasena what is reborn and he replies that it is mind and matter. 'Is it the same mind and matter that is reborn?' asks Milinda. Nāgasena replies,

> No, it is not, but by this mind and matter deeds are done and because of those deeds another mind and matter is reborn; but that mind and matter is not thereby released from the results of its previous deeds.... It is like a fire which a man might kindle and, having warmed himself, he might leave it burning and go away. Then if that fire were to set light to another man's field and the owner were to seize him and accuse him before the king, and he were to say, 'Your majesty, I did not set this man's field on fire. The fire that I left burning was different to that which burnt his field.'[74]

Just as the fire that burnt the neighbour's field depends on the original fire, so there is a conditioned relationship between one life and the next; they are not identical but neither are they completely distinct. The ephemeral nature of fire vividly illustrates this point. To fill out this idea still further, think of the relationship between an acorn and an oak. In dependence upon the acorn an oak tree grows, and yet no 'thing' passes from the acorn to the oak. At the same time, an oak cannot grow from nothing, nor can it grow from a chestnut; there is a relationship of *specific* conditionality between the acorn and the oak. An oak will grow in dependence upon the acorn given favourable conditions, yet the two are not the same. This simple example brings out something fundamentally mysterious and wonderful about all life: how do things evolve into other things? How are they related through time and space? These difficult questions are perhaps not fully answerable. Part of the problem is our tendency to think in terms of 'things' rather than conditions; we think that for rebirth to mean anything, there must be a thing (e.g. a soul) that passes from life to life, but perhaps this static model is inadequate. All the examples we have seen show that a relationship can exist between two 'things' such that the second arises in dependence upon the first, and yet no 'thing' passes between them.

The early Buddhist texts make it clear that there is no permanent consciousness that fares through the rounds of rebirth.[75] Consciousness is not an entity that exists independently of conditions that might somehow be 'transferred' to another body, instead it arises in dependence upon conditions. But if no 'thing' passes from life to life and there is only a relationship of dependent conditionality, is there *any* continuity across lives? Does it even make any sense to say that 'we' will be reborn?

It is sometimes said that it is our *saṃskāras* – our volitional tendencies – that are reborn. According to this view, we do not come into the world as a blank slate but have tendencies to act and think in particular ways. The temperament, interests, and values of children born within the same family can be strikingly different, and past lives may be offered as an explanation for this. Buddhism would fiercely deny Rousseau's declaration that 'Man is born free,' but speaking in terms of *saṃskāras* instead of a soul just places the problem at one remove. How is it that *saṃskāras* can be transferred from one psychophysical organism to another? Perhaps still more difficult to understand is how a being in one life can reap the consequences of the conduct of another who is now dead. How can an act committed in the past have consequences later down the line, even in the next life? What happens to it in between? What is the mechanism by which a bundle of tendencies transfers from association with one psychophysical organism to another?

Some of these questions were clearly problematic for the early Buddhists, and they came up with many wonderful – and sometimes weird – theories to account for them. One school, the Puggalavāda or 'Personalist', believed in a personal entity (*puggala*) that transmigrates from life to life and so provides the link of personal continuity that allows for karmas to act on an individual over time. This sounds remarkably like a soul, and, needless to say, the Personalists had their hands full defending themselves against such a charge. The medieval Pali scholar Buddhaghosa posited a 'rebirth-linking consciousness' (*paṭisandhi*), which connected the arising of a new life with the moment of death. But how one life stream can become associated with another is not made clear. Some schools were led to the conclusion that karmas continue to exist in some 'invisible' sense and adhere to a particular psychophysical continuum (a person) until they have worked out their consequences. They might be compared to dormant germs waiting to be activated and cause disease, though these germs were themselves seen as momentary and constantly giving rise to other germs almost identical to themselves.[76] Another school, the Sautrāntika, made use of a somewhat more poetic model to account for the process of karmic continuity. For them, each act 'perfumed' the individual and led to the planting of a 'seed' that would later germinate as good or bad *vipāka*.[77]

Such questions about the nature of personal continuity and karmic responsibility are difficult to answer because they raise fundamental philosophical questions about the nature of causal relationship, identity, and continuity. We seem capable of thinking only in terms of causal relations. According to the German philosopher Immanuel Kant, it is part of the fundamental structure of our consciousness to do so. We tend to think of one completely discrete thing acting upon another completely discrete thing and call this 'causation'. But causation is not something that is ever observed; it is an imagined relationship between two phenomena or events. Experience is a non-dual whole, which we analyse into 'cause' and 'effect', leaving us the problem of how to fit them together again. We see something change and conclude that something else 'caused' that change. But the world is not actually like that, and it is perhaps only by moving to a different level of experience that we can really begin to understand what rebirth may be getting at. Having said all this, the fact that we may neither fully understand how rebirth works nor be able to produce a workable model of it does not necessarily mean it has no meaning. Scientists still seem unable to explain how life occurs, how it is that a certain combination of tissues gives rise to an embryo, and yet we would not deny that it *does* occur.

This lack of certainty and understanding about experience can be very frustrating – even humiliating. But we can turn this experience to our advantage. If we are able to embrace our ignorance about such issues positively, we can move into a deeper experience of wonder at the mystery of being. We may also begin to realize that our attention will be better directed towards the practical questions of how to live our lives, rather than get caught up in metaphysical ones that may prove insoluble given the limitations of human experience. We must beware the danger of being hijacked by tantalizing metaphysical puzzles. The Buddha was very aware of this danger. One of his disciples, Mālunkyāputta, was troubled by such issues, which have been formulaically expressed in terms of the 'indeterminate questions'.[78] Is the world eternal? Is the world infinite? Is the soul identical with the body? Does the Buddha exist after death?[79]

Mālunkyāputta is dissatisfied that the Buddha has neither offered clear answers to these questions nor admitted he doesn't know the answers; he has simply left them 'undeclared'. So Mālunkyāputta works himself up into something of a rage and convinces himself that he is unwilling to carry on with spiritual practice unless the Buddha is willing to provide some answers.

He goes to the Buddha to have the matter out with him. 'If you know the answers to these questions,' he declares,' it should be simple for you to tell me. If you don't know the answers, just admit it.'

The Buddha responds by asking whether Mālunkyāputta has ever heard him offer to answer such questions. Mālunkyāputta admits that the Buddha had never done so. The Buddha then declares him to be a misguided man and introduces the famous parable of the poisoned arrow. Suppose a man were wounded by a poisoned arrow and his friends brought a surgeon to treat him. That man could say, 'I won't let the surgeon remove this arrow until I know who shot it, their clan name, whether they were tall or short, dark or light-skinned, what kind of bow was used, what feathers were used on the shaft,' and so on. This man would die, the Buddha declares, before getting answers to all his questions. In the same way, if anyone insists on knowing the answers to all the indeterminate questions before practising the spiritual life, they too will die before getting the answers.

The Buddha directs Mālunkyāputta's attention to the reality of suffering (the wound). He points out that pursuing the undetermined questions does not lead to spiritual awakening. Instead, reflecting on the four noble truths – suffering, the cause of suffering, the end of suffering, and the path leading to the end of suffering – is a more profitable subject for reflection which will lead us to spiritual release. The Buddha directs attention away from metaphysical questions to the practical concerns of human existence: the reality of suffering and the need to transcend it. This perhaps suggests that what we believe with regard to rebirth is of less importance than whether we awaken to the reality of our human condition and take steps to transcend it. Buddhism is a spiritual tradition that emphasizes practice and transformation above belief and faith.

8

THE SIX REALMS

Buddhism adopted the view that the nature of our rebirth is consistent with the kind of life we have lived. The kind of *saṃskāras* we have developed over the course of one life is said to shape who we will become in future. But not only do our karmas shape the mental landscape of our future life, they even shape the kind of world we will be born into. This needs explaining. According to traditional Buddhist cosmology, there are five or six principal realms (*gati*) into which beings can be reborn.[80] These are the realms of the gods, humans, *asuras* or angry gods, *pretas* or 'hungry ghosts', hell beings, and the animals (fig. 7). These realms are divided into two classes: the *sugati* or favourable realms, which comprise the human and god realms, and the *duggati* or unfavourable realms, which comprise the rest. All beings transmigrate from realm to realm depending on the quality of their lives; we are engaged in a deadly serious version of snakes and ladders. If we live a skilful life we will go to one of the *sugati*, otherwise we are destined for the *duggati*.

While the god realm is believed to be the most pleasurable, the human realm is the most desirable because it offers a unique opportunity for spiritual evolution. Within the human realm there is enough suffering to provoke beings into examining their

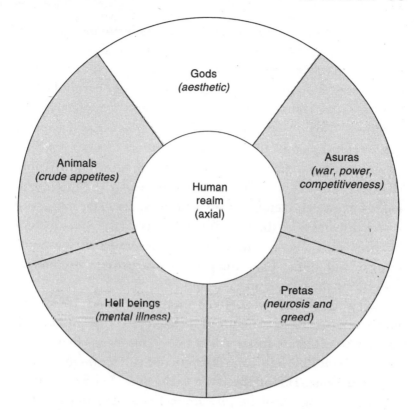

FIG. 7: THE SIX REALMS

lives and looking for the means to transcend it, but enough pleasure to prevent them being crushed by the pain of their predicament. This enables them to develop awareness of their overall
condition and to exercise choice, rather than simply react to
pleasure with craving and to pain with aversion. The human
realm is then an *axial* realm, the most auspicious realm for spiritual awakening.

All the other realms have acute limitations in relation to spiritual awakening. In the animal realm beings are completely
absorbed in eating, sleeping, and reproducing. They have no
self-awareness, no concept of spiritual evolution, and hence no

possibility of bringing it about. In the hell realm beings are so weighed down by their sufferings they lose all perspective, inevitably spiralling down into deeper and deeper misery as their pain causes them to think and act in increasingly harmful ways. The gods are intoxicated by pleasure and completely self-absorbed. They live in a dream world where everything comes easily; consequently they pay no attention to their spiritual progress or the welfare of others. They have no thought of ever changing. The angry gods are constantly at war. They are dominated by competitiveness, greed, and ambition. Their sole desire is acquisitiveness, so they have no thoughts for the development of their spirit. Finally, the pretas are consumed by insatiable hunger and thirst. Everything they eat turns to excrement, everything they drink turns to liquid fire.

Owing to the unfavourable conditions found in all the non-human realms, pretas are more likely to compound unskilful *saṃskāras* than to foster skilful ones. This means that once a being falls into a lower realm it is very difficult for them to move to a higher one. This applies even to the gods. Even while their experience is exquisitely pleasurable, the attachments they develop are likely to lead them into states of craving, possibly resulting in rebirth in the preta realms.

In view of all this, the human realm is seen as highly desirable and supremely precious, because it offers uniquely favourable conditions for attaining spiritual awakening. There is a traditional reflection that encourages us to appreciate this. We should imagine a lonely old turtle – a turtle seemingly as old as the great ocean in which he lives – so old, in fact, that he has become blind and can swim only with great labour. Imagine also that floating aimlessly like a piece of driftwood, upon that same vast, deep, and mysterious ocean, is a battered round yoke with a hole through it. Every hundred years the blind turtle pokes his head above the surface of the water. How likely is it that it will push its head up through the yoke? Such an outcome would not only be highly improbable but miraculous. But according to Buddhist tradition such an outcome is more probable than a human birth. This parable aims to show us how truly rare is the human birth and, in view of this, that it should be supremely cherished.[81]

But is it really possible for us to be reborn into these other realms? Can a being, once human, really degenerate to the level of an animal? Can a human being become, for instance, a locust? Traditional Buddhism approaches this quite literally, but we might feel unable to do so. Given the modern scientific understanding of life and evolution, we might be inclined to think that once it has attained self-consciousness it would be difficult for a being to slip back into animal consciousness. If this sort of degeneration were possible, we must beware of thinking that a human consciousness could become trapped in, say, a hamster's body. Any animal will have a degree of consciousness consistent with its nature.

We have already seen that Karma applies only to beings that have developed self-consciousness and are capable of moral discrimination. This seems to imply that the animal realm is one of pure effect. Animals do not sow karma; they simply reap. But this creates a problem for the traditional Buddhist model. How does a being in the animal realm get out of it again? There seem to be two possibilities. The first is that when the karma that led to the animal rebirth is exhausted, the effects of other karmas will come into play, leading to birth in a different realm. The second possibility is that, through the assistance of an external influence (such as a compassionate Buddha), animals can develop self-awareness and transcend their bestial nature.

How do beings break out of the other realms? The inhabitants of the god realm rest on their laurels; their happiness depends on their previous good conduct. As in the animal realm, their state seems to be a fairly passive one, albeit enjoyable. Owing to their self-absorbed complacency, they eventually exhaust their merit and 'fall' to the human realm. The landing is often bumpy. The angry gods are so driven by their envy of the gods, so intoxicated by their thirst for power and possession, that it is unlikely they will ever act skilfully. If this realm is one where karma is created, then it is most likely that they will fall into an even worse existence, probably hell. And as far as the pretas and hell beings are concerned, it is difficult to see how they could ever emerge from their uncharitable domains. The pretas are so dominated by craving that they will constantly act unskilfully in order to alleviate their hunger and thirst, while the hell beings are so locked into a cycle of suffering that they are most likely to spiral deeper and deeper into their dark and miserable pit. After all, it's difficult to remain positive when you are being forced to swallow red-hot iron balls and your hands and feet are pierced with red-hot iron stakes, not to mention being made to climb up and down a great mound of burning coals or cooked in a red-hot cauldron.[82]

It may be that all the realms (except the human) are best understood as passive states of *vipāka*, in which beings simply reap the fruits of their karma from previous lives. If so, once their residents have exhausted their karma they will move to a higher realm. But if this is not so they are likely to depend on outside help to pull them from their dreadful state. In the human realm, on other hand, beings can make choices and create new *saṃskāras*; they can direct their own lives and improve their future. Rather than depending on some outside agency, human beings can 'save' themselves – but they can also 'damn' themselves too.

A Psychological Reading of the Six Realms

So far we have approached the six realms at face value, understanding them in the literal way of Buddhist tradition as possible
worlds into which we may be born. But much can be gained
through reading them symbolically, as a range of mental states –
or personal worlds – that human beings can inhabit. Accordingly, the god realm is one of extreme sensuous enjoyment, aesthetic satisfaction, success, happiness, even intoxication. In such
a state we are blissed out but blind to some harsh realities: death,
the suffering of others, and the concealment of suffering we
require for our continued happiness, such as the poverty of
those who provide us with cheap goods. In a sense, then, the
god realm is one of deliberate ignorance of the dark side of life,
an eternal, adolescent, good-time attitude. As Tennyson puts it,

> For they lie beside their nectar, and the bolts are hurl'd
> Far below them in the valleys, and all the clouds are lightly
>   curl'd
> Round their golden houses, girdled with the gleaming
>   world.[83]

The gods fly high, so high that they manage to avoid seeing the
suffering and pain below them. But they will inevitably crash,
and when this happens it is often very messy; a fallen god is a
sad creature indeed.

When we live in the animal realm, we simply act out our biological and instinctive urges. We have little or no imagination,
no direction, no despair, but no hope either. We are controlled
by our desires and never transcend them. We are mechanical,
not making free choices or fresh decisions, just swimming
around like goldfish in a bowl, driven by vaguely conscious impulses of craving and aversion. So we have no freedom, no
choice, no creativity. This is probably the condition in which we
spend most of our lives.

The preta realm is characterized by extreme neurotic desire. We have a constant feeling of need, of hunger, of emptiness. We perpetually look for something to satisfy our sense of lack – relationships, work, possessions, even religion – but nothing ever does. As soon as we acquire what we want, new desires arise. We are never content. This is because we expect more from things than they can give us. This seems to be the condition of the modern consumer and it is a condition encouraged by our desire-oriented society, presumably because it is this neurotic desire that drives the wheels of capitalism. Consumer capitalism seems to be founded on the lie that through acquisition we become happier. So instead of taking care of ourselves and addressing our spiritual hunger we look to external things to fill our inner lack, in the belief that if we stuff ourselves full of experiences, possessions, ideas, and sexual partners we will alleviate our hunger. While there is nothing wrong with these things in themselves and only a killjoy would deny that they bring a certain degree of happiness, our spiritual nature will not find fulfilment in this way. This is why our craving returns more ferociously than before. Probably no one believes that physical hunger can be relieved by buying a new car – we need to eat – yet we make the same kind of mistake in other contexts, believing, for instance, that buying more clothes can alleviate our spiritual emptiness. This is the nature of the futile and desperate activity of the preta being.

The realm of the angry gods is one of extreme jealousy, competitiveness, anger, and frustration. In illustrations of this realm, the angry gods are shown at war with the gods, battling to gain possession of the wish-fulfilling tree. As long as someone else has something they don't, the angry gods are never satisfied – they must have it as well or preferably *instead*. They would even prefer to destroy it than have someone else enjoy it. So they are never happy. The joy of others is painful to them; it affronts their megalomaniac desire to control all power and all pleasure. It is something like this perverse attitude that, in *Othello*, drives Iago to destroy his captain's happiness. For the angry gods, the purpose of the world is exclusively to satisfy their own desires – other people are either obstacles to their happiness or instruments by which it can be achieved. They are supremely self-centred.

Hell beings are overwhelmed by suffering, a suffering that makes them unable to appreciate or enjoy any pleasures. They are unable to think of others because the intensity of their suffering absorbs all their energy. Their unbearable pain makes them lash out violently in all directions, unaware that they harm others by so doing. They are unable to imagine the suffering of others because their sensibilities are so distorted by their pain. So they live in a very isolated world dominated by nightmares, horror, fear, and desperation. Conditions such as paranoid schizophrenia exemplify this kind of experience all too graphically.

As I have already suggested, the human realm is understood to be axial. It is perhaps the most objective of the states. Human beings are able to relate to their experience with clarity and understanding. They recognize that they experience both joy and suffering (and a raft of other emotions) but these experiences don't intoxicate or depress them. They feel the weight and force of their habits but have sufficient awareness to resist them. Human beings are awake to the spiritual dimension of their lives and are motivated to explore it.

In reflecting on these descriptions, we may begin to wonder whether any of the non-human realms correspond to our own experience of life. While it is likely that we will feel an affinity with one or more of the non-human realms, it is unlikely that we will be totally embroiled in any one of them. If we were, a book of this kind would not interest us. We could think of ourselves as constantly moving from realm to realm, perhaps with one realm representing our basic or predominant experience. Using this model of the realms might enable us to gain a novel perspective on our lives and identify which features of our lifestyle need to be addressed and transformed. In transforming them we create the possibility of truly human consciousness, which provides the basis for lasting spiritual transformation.

Getting Out of the Realms

I suggested earlier that once in one of the lower realms it might be very difficult to climb out again. So, having fallen, are we condemned to eternal suffering? If our own actions were the only factors that shaped the pilgrimage of our lives then this might be so, but fortunately we participate in a world with other beings whose own self-willed actions influence the working out of our lives for better or worse. Traditional representations of the six realms show a Buddha in each who offers appropriate help to the needy. In the god realm appears a white Buddha with a lute, playing the melody of impermanence. In the realm of the angry gods, a green Buddha brandishes a sword of spiritual wisdom. In the preta realm, a red Buddha offers food and drink. In the hell realm a smoke-coloured Buddha offers a soothing balm. In the animal realm appears a blue Buddha with a book. Finally, a yellow Buddha dressed as a monk appears in the human realm, exemplifying a spiritual life.

The six Buddhas symbolize the activity of compassion – the loving and practical response to the suffering of others. It is worth noting that only in the human realm does a Buddha directly offer spiritual teachings. Often the help that beings need is much more basic. A starving man needs to be fed before being taught the Dharma. Occasionally, though, beings in extreme suffering are able to embrace extreme solutions, solutions that catapult them into a dramatically expanded world of possibilities from which they never look back. This sometimes happens in the case of a religious conversion. More often, though, the solution itself turns out to be just a new kind of box, and when the bottom falls out of it they plunge deeper into despair than before. This shows that it is not necessarily easy to help people because they first need insight into the root of their difficulties. For this reason, Buddhist compassion is underpinned by wisdom.

While there is a sense, then, in which we are on our own, responsible for our actions, heirs to our karma, there is also a sense in which we are all in it together: life is a collective enterprise. This allows amazing new possibilities. We can both help others to transform themselves and be helped by others to transform ourselves. This awareness can lead both to a profound sense of gratitude that other beings can – and often do – help us, and a potent sense of our own capacity – and responsibility – for relieving the suffering of others. We live in an interdependent world and a truly creative life is one in which we not only take individual responsibility but also learn to live interdependently with others, recognizing that they can both enhance and diminish the quality of our lives and that we can do the same for them.

9

BORN AGAIN

While all Buddhist traditions seem to accept some notion of rebirth, there is no unified view about precisely how events unfold after the moment of death. Theravāda Buddhism generally asserts that rebirth is immediate; there is no intermediate realm (*antarābhava*). The Tibetan schools, on the other hand, hold to the notion of a *bardo* (intermediate state) before rebirth takes place, which can last up to forty-nine days, and this has led to the development of a unique literature, even a 'science' of death and rebirth, a good deal of which is set down in what is popularly known as *The Tibetan Book of the Dead*.[84] The philosophical foundation for all this is found in earlier Buddhist scholasticism.

While Theravāda Buddhism generally denies there is an intermediate state, there is some evidence in early Buddhist texts which seems to support the idea.[85] One early school that adopted this view was called the Sarvāstivāda, and it was this tradition that gave rise to the conception of a *bardo*. The Sarvāstivādins believed that between death and rebirth there is another kind of existence comprising a 'body' of five *skandhas*, a sort of limbo in which beings do not yet reap the consequences of their previous actions (this happens only when they undergo rebirth) but in which they may still influence their future bourn. The death process and the intermediate state is believed to offer a uniquely favourable opportunity for spiritual awakening. The origins of this view can be found in early Buddhist scriptures.[86]

The intermediate state being was known as the *gandharva*,[87] and it was believed that, for an embryo to implant itself in a womb, not only were biological conditions needed but the presence of a *gandharva* ready to take rebirth was also required. The form of the *gandharva* was believed to be consistent with the form of the kind of being that would be reborn, so, for example, the *gandharva* would have a human form if it was heading for a human rebirth. The intermediate being is the size of a five-year-old child but with fully developed organs. Some more modest intermediate beings are fully dressed, whereas others are naked and can be seen only by other intermediate beings belonging to the same class or with the benefit of the Divine Eye.[88] An intermediate being cannot be turned away from its intended realm of rebirth, even by force. It is nourished by odours: a *gandharva* of low rank lives on unpleasant smells, while one of high rank lives on pleasant ones. There seems to be a range of views on how long the intermediate state lasts. One view is that it lasts just as long as the *gandharva* cannot find the necessary conditions for its rebirth.

The explanation of how rebirth actually takes place is interesting. The mind, troubled by defilements, is propelled towards rebirth through its desire for sex. The intermediate being possesses the Divine Eye and uses it to see the place of rebirth, where it witnesses its potential father and mother in sexual union, which troubles it. If the *gandharva* is male, he experiences lust for his mother and hatred towards the father, whom he sees as a rival. If the *gandharva* is female, she experiences sexual desire for the father and aversion towards the mother. This explanation is perhaps an intriguing anticipation of some of

Freud's developmental ideas. Modern technologies, such as conception through *in vitro* fertilization and cloning, would seem difficult to accommodate into this account. Through its desire for sex, the mind attaches itself to the place where the sexual organs are joined, imagining that it is uniting with the mother (if male) or father (if female). The intermediate being then installs itself in the womb until birth takes place. It seems that not all beings enter the womb conscious of what they are doing; some think to themselves, 'The wind blows, the heavens rain; it is cold,... people are in an uproar,' and enter the womb believing it to be a shelter. Before they know it they find themselves thrown into the world.

Death and Rebirth in Tibetan Buddhism

The Tibetan schools place great importance on the death bardo because they believe it provides a precious opportunity for spiritual awakening. For this reason, a good deal of their spiritual practice is geared towards preparing for it so that the death experience can be put to best use. Spiritual practice as a whole could well be described as a preparation for death. As we approach death, images of our past deeds supposedly flash across our minds. For instance, if our life has been skilful, then skilful volitions are most likely to be present at the time of death and lead to a favourable rebirth. These schools believe that in the bardo we are confronted by the white light of reality, which is nothing other than the true nature of our mind, but instead of recognizing it as such we become frightened and fall into a swoon. At first, we don't even realize we have died. We then undergo a series of experiences in which we are confronted by reality in the guise of different Buddha and Bodhisattva forms. These experiences offer us a series of opportunities to wake up to reality, but without adequate preparation we are likely to misunderstand their true nature, become terrified by the appearance of the angelic figures, and scuttle towards the nearest womb.

The Tibetan Book of the Dead could be described as an instruction manual for the living so that they can help the deceased to orient themselves through the death experience and attain spiritual liberation rather than rebirth. It describes in great detail the parade of Enlightened figures that will confront us in the after-death state. Over a series of 'days', we will be faced with a choice between the startling light of reality as manifested through various Buddha figures and the dull light of rebirth that emanates from each of the six realms. The light of the Buddhas is intense, so bright that it frightens us, whereas the lights emanating from each of the six realms are dull and soothing. If we have an affinity with the god realm we are likely to be drawn to its dull white light. Similarly, the angry god realm emits a dull red light, the human realm dull blue, the animal realm dull green, the preta realm dull yellow, and finally the hell realm emits a dull smoke-coloured light.

If we are able to embrace the light of reality, we may gain spiritual awakening in the bardo state; if not, then we will seek re-embodiment in whichever realm we feel most affinity with. One way of preparing for our encounter with the startling light of reality is therefore through regular meditation on a Bodhisattva or Buddha figure. During the first few days, the deceased is confronted by a series of peaceful Buddha figures whose beauty and purity may be so terrifying that they swoon again. As time passes, the deities that appear become more wrathful in aspect and in conventional appearance seem demonic, though they are traditionally believed to be less frightening than the peaceful figures.

It is considered important to remind the departing spirit of the Three Jewels – the Buddha, the Dharma, and the Sangha – as he or she enters the intermediate state. For this reason, it is usual to place images of Buddhas around the dying person, to recite mantras, and even to read instructions from *The Tibetan Book of the Dead*. By doing this, the chances of the dying person recognizing what is happening to them as they enter the bardo and responding positively to the experience are greatly improved.

But the teaching of the bardo also has a more immediate, everyday relevance. Not only is death a valuable bardo; daily life also represents a continuing opportunity to embrace the light of reality. At every moment we can choose to understand and live according to truth, or reject the truth and perpetuate our delusion and evasion. At every moment we have a choice whether to embrace compassion, clarity, and equanimity or to reinforce petty selfishness, vagueness, and partiality. We don't need to wait until the moment of death to experience the clear light of reality – it is present before us even now. It is through making this choice that we can begin to redirect the course of our lives and create a different future. Rather than be directed by what is worst in us, we can deliberately align our will with what is best and break free of the gravitational pull of unskilful habits.

The Transference of Consciousness

In addition to general spiritual training as a preparation for death, there is also a specific practice that involves developing the ability to transfer one's consciousness at the moment of death (*phowa*). The aim of this practice is to be able to project one's consciousness into the Pure Land – an ideal place for spiritual awakening. One version of this practice aims to train the practitioner to reach the Pure Land of Maitreya, the future Buddha.[89] It involves visualizing Maitreya's Pure Land and invoking Maitreya. One then engages in a visualization practice wherein one is purified by him. Then one visualizes a mystic drop that shoots up from one's heart to the crown of one's head. This drop is visualized as the embodiment of one's mind and subtle energies, and it is this that is ejected at the point of death. The main aim of the practice is to identify oneself fully with Maitreya, and to this extent it is much like other practices that involve the visualization of deities.

Consciousness is projected out of the body with the help of a special mantric formula, the syllable *hik*, and can be brought back again using the syllable *phat*. One knows that one has become adept at this practice when a small blister appears on one's head that emits a little blood and pus. This is the preparatory practice. When one notices signs of death approaching, one prepares to eject one's consciousness and has to make sure that one does so before death actually occurs, otherwise one will be reborn in the ordinary way. It has been reported that a number of Tibetan monks imprisoned by the Chinese killed themselves by ejecting their consciousness in this way.[90]

This may all seem rather remote and esoteric – it certainly does to me – but a simple principle can be seen to underlie it: if we live an engaged spiritual life, we can look upon death calmly because we have nothing to fear. Our best 'insurance' against rebirth is spiritual awakening in this life. In order to avoid being carried away by exotic, technical practices we may do well to bear this constantly in mind.

The Tulku System

While the aim of Buddhist practice in general has always been to escape from the round of rebirth (*saṃsāra*), some remarkable beings, out of compassion for the world and a desire to help others to liberate themselves, are believed to have the ability to deliberately engineer their own rebirths, even though they themselves are already spiritually freed. This principle is embodied in the tulku system of Tibet, an ecclesiastical structure that may be unique in world history. The Tibetan Buddhist tradition bases its model of spiritual life on the ideal of the Bodhisattva, the 'awakening being', who not only wants to gain spiritual awakening in order to be free of suffering but also wants all other beings to share that liberation. The Bodhisattva is committed to helping all beings to liberate themselves before he or she can think of resting. Clearly this is an endless task. The Bodhisattva embodies the principle of compassion, the inexhaustible urge to help beings transcend their suffering. This is how the tulkus of Tibet are seen. So figures such as the Dalai Lama, the Karmapa, and others are seen as manifestations of Bodhisattvas. The Dalai Lama is, for instance, seen as an embodiment of the mythic Bodhisattva Avalokiteśvara, who is sometimes depicted with eleven heads in order that he may see all the sufferings of beings, and a thousand hands so that he may reach out and respond to those needs.

After the death of a tulku, especially one who has held an influential or important office, his re-embodiment is usually sought out. This involves relying on oracles, divinations, and even clues left by the departing tulku. When a potential candidate is identified, he (and it is almost invariably he) is subjected to rigorous tests, such as presentation with several rosaries (*mālas*) to see if he picks up the one that belonged to the previous tulku. If the candidate passes all the tests he is authenticated and normally taken at an early age – perhaps as young as four – to be trained at the appropriate monastery. Any important responsibilities he held in his previous life will gradually be handed back to him, as well as his land and other property.

While this process might seem bizarre, it is in fact only following through some of the logical implications of the teaching on rebirth. If rebirth does happen, and particularly if advanced beings can consciously direct their rebirth, it should be possible to identify those rebirths. Unfortunately this system, like any other, is open to abuse, and it has recently resulted in the independent enthronement of rival candidates by different political factions. In the case of the appointment of the most recent Karmapa – the head of the Kagyu sect – this has even led to violent confrontations between opposing groups. In reality there has probably always been a certain amount of political manoeuvring and even skulduggery in the recognition of tulkus.

Until recent decades, all tulkus were either Tibetan or Mongolian, but since the diaspora, a number of Tibetan tulkus are believed to have been reborn in Western families, perhaps the best known of whom is Lama Osel, who has been 'confirmed' as the reincarnation of Lama Yeshe and was born of Spanish parents.[91] Some of these tulkus have undergone traditional Tibetan Buddhist training.

The issue of tulkus and their status has become somewhat controversial in recent decades since some authenticated tulkus (that is, 'living Bodhisattvas') have acted in ways contrary to the spirit of Buddhism. While some of their supporters defend this kind of activity as 'crazy wisdom', it should perhaps best serve to warn us that spiritual teachers should not necessarily be judged on the basis of claims made about or even by them, but rather in themselves. What does it matter if someone is a bona fide tulku if they live unskilfully? This kind of possibility should alert us to potential weaknesses in the tulku system and encourage us to beware of trusting status or title as an index of attainment.

A further feature of the tulku system that may also be unique in the world's religions is the concept of *multiple* rebirths, a possibility portrayed in Bernardo Bertolucci's film *Little Buddha*: a Tibetan lama takes *three* Western rebirths, including one as a girl (highly unusual). In principle, a high lama is believed to be capable of giving rise to as many as *five* rebirths. These comprise the body, speech, and mind manifestations together with the karma and *guṇa* (meaning 'quality') manifestations. It is, though, highly unusual for five reincarnations of the same tulku to be recognized, and even in cases where multiple rebirths have come to light, one rebirth is usually considered to be the 'main' incarnation. The concept of multiple rebirths raises important questions and possibilities for the teaching of rebirth as a whole, some of which we will look at later.

10

THE EVIDENCE FOR
REBIRTH

There have always been people who claim to remember their past lives, often in thoroughly romantic circumstances. With the rise of Theosophy in the late-nineteenth century, for instance, sensational claims by individuals who believed themselves, centuries ago, to have been Egyptian pharaohs or ancient queens became something of a minor craze. But while many of us would perhaps like to believe that our ancestry is noble and distinguished, not to say exotic, rather than constituting reliable evidence, stories like this suggest wish fulfilment and escapism. Outlandish past-life claims have no doubt undermined rather than enhanced any credibility that the notion of rebirth might deserve. This may at least partly explain why it has become a belief more associated with fantasists and cranks than with trustworthy thinkers.

Before going any further, we must recognize that talking about claims of past lives raises terminological difficulties. Many people use the terms 'rebirth' and 'reincarnation' interchangeably, but they are technically distinct. Buddhist doctrine affirms rebirth (as I have described it in previous chapters) *as opposed to reincarnation*. The key difference is that reincarnation is associated with the notion of an unchanging essence that is 'reincarnated' life after life. The Buddhist position is more paradoxical: it states that there *is* rebirth, but there is no *one* who is reborn. Looking at the evidence for rebirth demands that we speak of previous lives; as in 'I will be reborn', etc. These turns of phrase can easily be read as – and prehaps slip into a belief in– an identity that carries on from life to life, and thus a belief that 'I' will survive, even that we are eternal. This is something Buddhism denies.

If we think in terms of images, reincarnation can be likened to a string of beads, each life being linked by the same thread: a soul or identity that carries on. Rebirth, on the other hand, can be compared to a pile of coins, each coin stacked on the next, and conditioned by its place in the pile – by what has gone before – but with no unchanging thread connecting them.

Bearing this distinction in mind, we can look at some of the more reputable evidence in favour of rebirth. In doing so, we should note that impartial evidence is scant. This can be explained partly by the fact that few investigators have been sufficiently motivated to examine thoroughly the cases that have come to light. Since the available evidence is relatively complex, highly ambiguous, and raises many further questions, this is not the place for a thorough review of it, but there are, even so, some issues worth noting.

Research on past lives tends to fall into three categories: children's claims of past-life memories, birthmark matches, and past-life regression of adults. The last seems to have been the most unreliable. One example of past-life regression is the Bridey Murphy case of the 1950s – made famous in a book and film – in which Virginia Tighe, a woman from Colorado, was hypnotized and subsequently 'remembered' the life of a nineteenth-century woman from Cork, in Ireland.[92] While under hypnosis, she talked in an Irish brogue, sang Irish songs, and remembered being held as she bent to kiss the Blarney Stone. No nineteenth-century Irishwoman corresponding to Bridey Murphy was ever identified, but one newspaper found a Bridie Murphey Corkell in twentieth-century Wisconsin. It turned out that this woman had lived across the street from where Virginia Tighe grew up. What Virginia reported while hypnotized were not recollections of a previous life but highly embroidered memories from her childhood. While not all cases of past-life regression are so easily debunked, even the most plausible evidence of this sort often describes a life for which there are few historical records. This means that many of the subject's statements about the alleged previous personality are not verifiable.

The one man who has perhaps done more than any other to investigate rebirth systematically and put rebirth theory on the map of the scientifically credible is Dr Ian Stevenson. Stevenson has written many books recording the thousands of cases of alleged rebirth experiences he has investigated.[3] His cases are far from sensationalistic: his witnesses don't tend to recall lives in which they were important or romantic figures but quite ordinary people, usually belonging to the same community as themselves.

Typically, a child will begin talking about a dead individual (the 'previous personality' or PP) at quite an early age, usually between two and five, and generally stop between the ages of five and eight, though not always. Sometimes they talk about a deceased friend or relative, but in other cases the PP is unknown to the host family. The child might insist on being taken 'home', that is, to the PP's home. It is often claimed that the child recognized the PP's family and friends without prompting, and had other knowledge about the PP that he or she could not have obtained through normal means. As if to underline their statements, some children bear birthmarks that allegedly correspond to wounds suffered by the PP and which are sometimes confirmed by postmortem reports. The child might also demonstrate behaviours associated with the life of the PP, such as a phobia relating to the way the PP had died.

In *Old Souls*, Tom Shroder, a journalist, records his encounters with Stevenson as he accompanied the scientist on field trips to investigate past-life memories.[94] Initially very sceptical, Shroder's instinctive materialism was strongly challenged by the various witnesses he encountered in Lebanon and India.

Stevenson's research shows several common features among people who claim to remember past lives. First of all, such cases are much more plentiful among communities where rebirth or reincarnation is widely accepted. A sceptic might suggest that, within such a community, past-life memories are in some sense manufactured, though it is possible that the reality gave rise to the belief rather than the other way around. There are many fewer cases of past-life memories among Western subjects. This might be because such memories, if they manifest, are not taken seriously so children quickly learn to suppress them. But it is worth noting that such cases are not unknown.

Secondly, many children who claim to remember their past lives recall having died in violent or tragic circumstances. If the memories are genuine, this could indicate that serious trauma interrupts the usual process of forgetting that enables other people to begin a new life unencumbered by disturbing memories of the past that may lead to identity confusion. In at least some cases, though, it may be that a seemingly dramatic past-life experience functions as a way of recording current life traumas that are too difficult to face directly.

In a number of Stevenson's cases, the subjects identify at least as strongly with their previous personality as with their present one, sometimes so much so that they find the memories upsetting or yearn to be with the family of their PP. This seems to have led, in some instances, to something of a personality crisis, when an individual has felt more affinity with their alleged previous life than with their current one. In one case, a child born as a Muslim claimed he came from a Hindu family and refused to follow Muslim customs. Since Islam rejects the notion of rebirth, this case is particularly interesting and difficult to explain as fraud. Far from gaining from the situation, the family were embarrassed by it and badly inconvenienced. Cases such as this illustrate that if rebirth is a common event, there is good reason for having some mechanism that suppresses past-life memories to avoid this kind of confusion and distress. This could explain why so few people retain such memories.

A third point of interest is the time gap between the death of the alleged PP and the birth of the current one. The average interval in Stevenson's cases is about eight months. This implies that the PP 'enters' the foetus at a relatively late stage of development and certainly not at the point of conception. The prevailing Buddhist view would, I think, suggest that consciousness joins the fertilized egg at the point of conception. If it is true that the personality joins the growing foetus at a relatively late stage, does it have consciousness before this? Without the intervention of another personality seeking rebirth, would the foetus survive? Or is there a 'default' personality that would develop anyway?

Finally, as we have been learning, Buddhist tradition asserts that the status of our current life is dependent on our moral conduct in previous ones. But Shroder noted that in the cases he witnessed,

> the relation between the two lives seemed random and naturalistic, the way that the location of an oak seedling might relate to the century-old tree from which the acorn fell – governed by proximity, wind currents, and chance, not moral order.[95]

A traditional Buddhist might explain this discrepancy by suggesting that what governed the current rebirth might have been another life before the most proximate one. There is no way to prove or disprove this.

Shroder's personal conclusions after his travels with Stevenson are worth noting. His previous, somewhat sceptical, materialism was deeply shaken by the people he encountered, though this does not mean that he came to accept the evidence at face value. To think in terms of one personality being reincarnated as another is, he believes, too simplistic and linear a model to explain what is going on.

> These children are less important for what they say about the specifics of what happens after we die, than for what they say about how the world works – that it's mysterious, that there are larger forces at work, that – in some way – we're all connected by forces beyond our understanding – but definitely not irrelevant to our lives.[96]

The evidence that exists in support of rebirth is certainly not compelling, but at least some it of it is plausible and hard to explain using established knowledge. While sceptics might point to the large number of cases that have been shown to be fraudulent, this does not account for all the available evidence. Other explanations have included cryptomnesia, when someone has learned about someone else's life but forgets they have done so; genetic memory, a speculative theory that the memories of parents and grandparents are somehow genetically encoded in their children; and retrocognition, when someone has extra- sensory access to memories of past events.

Several of these explanations – some even advanced by scientists – seem no less outlandish or implausible than rebirth. One of the reasons some observers have resorted to these explanations is the lack of any model for a mechanism that could explain how rebirth might come about. This seems to encourage what may be an unreasonable prejudice against the belief, but the available evidence suggests that, despite the lack of a plausible model, it would not seem unreasonable to believe in rebirth in a more literal sense; at the same time, someone who does not accept it could not be accused of refusing to face incontrovertible facts.

This, then, puts the ball back in the individual's court. Whether we adopt rebirth as a belief or not is our own choice. But perhaps more important than this is to ask ourselves why we want to accept or reject it and what implications our belief has for the way that we live our lives now.

Perhaps the most honest response would be agnostic: we don't really know – though on emotive issues like this it is not always easy to remain impartial because the weight of our conditioning tends to draw us in one direction or another. The truth is that even if we were to accept the small number of cases that suggest someone has been reborn, this does not mean that we will also be reborn, because there is no evidence that is even remotely compelling that suggests that *everyone* will be reborn.

So if we don't really know whether or not we will be reborn, where are we left? This state of uncertainty throws us back to the reality of *this* life and the urgent need to address the way we are living *now*; there can be no guarantee about what the future will bring. What we do know is that we are recreating ourselves day by day and building a world that accords with our habits. The bulk of our attention should surely be directed at the concrete, practical questions and dilemmas of daily life, rather than the ultimately unanswerable puzzles of a potential afterlife. Are we creating for ourselves – and for others – a better life or a worse one? We must beware of speculation about rebirth becoming a distraction from our fundamental responsibility to live now.

11

MAKING SOME SENSE OF IT

I t is one thing to describe how Buddhism has traditionally understood the process of rebirth, and even identify how this understanding has become embodied in forms of practice and organization like the tulku system, but it is quite another to be able to accept it all. Does rebirth as expounded by the Buddhist tradition make any useful sense? Is it self-contradictory? Is it just make-believe? In this chapter I want to address some of these questions and in doing so expand the possibilities of what rebirth could mean. Before doing this, I want to draw attention to a few of the problems that Western people might have in engaging with notions of rebirth, particularly if they have come to understand the world of human beings in the context of evolution.

Rebirth and Evolution

The ancient Indian lived in a cyclical cosmos in which nothing much ever changed. He or she had no historical sense; no idea that culture, religion, and technology were things that might evolve. He or she seemingly believed in a mythic universe with Mount Meru at its centre surrounded by four continents, one of which was our world. Naturally, 'our world' didn't extend much beyond India; it certainly didn't include Australia or America, for example. Man had always been around and always would be.

Importantly, the ancient Indian did not encounter Darwin's ideas about the evolution of species. The emergence of the theory of evolution has revolutionized how humanity thinks of itself and its origins. In the Europe of the Middle Ages, most people believed human beings were unique creations, made in God's own image and set completely apart from the animal kingdom. In modern times, the paradigm of evolution is difficult to resist, and while it certainly doesn't provide all the answers, some of its basic insights have become part of the fabric of how we think about ourselves. This is important for the doctrine of rebirth.

We have seen that rebirth in the traditional, individualized sense can only properly be talked about in relation to beings with self-consciousness, since only such beings are capable of moral discrimination. If this is true, rebirth must have emerged with the dawning of self-consciousness, something that happened fairly recently. How and why did rebirth start to emerge at this point? How does the notion of the continuity of life after death sit alongside evolution?

There are further questions which a rebirth theory needs to address. For instance, why are there now more human beings than there used to be? If one death gives rise to one rebirth, how is it that the population has been dramatically rising for the last two centuries? Should we not have the same number of people? A traditional answer might be that beings are reborn from other realms. A more recent proposal has suggested that the population explosion is not incompatible with rebirth if the time spent in the after-death state is not constant. This theory posits that in the past a human-type consciousness might only have been reborn, say, every thousand years or so, but is now likely to be reborn more quickly.[97] If this explanation is plausible, what might be its cause?

There might even be a more 'cosmic' explanation. It could be that there are now more individualized consciousnesses than there used to be. Some thinkers, including Hegel, believed that history reveals a progressive manifestation of consciousness (or spirit) and therefore evolution has a direction: the complete manifestation of self-consciousness.

Having noted some of the difficulties that can arise in approaching rebirth from a world-view strongly influenced by the theory of evolution, I want now to look at some broader questions that arise in relation to making sense of what rebirth could be getting at. My aim is to explore how rebirth ideas could enable us to live more creatively.

Is Rebirth a Linear Process?

The traditional model of rebirth suggests we are reborn lifetime after lifetime, but if the doctrine of *anātman* is true what sense can it make to say 'we' are reborn? We are changing all the time, albeit slowly, and over several lifetimes – not to speak of hundreds – we will no doubt change significantly. So what relationship could there be between me and my 'ancestor-me' one hundred generations ago? Sometimes I find it difficult to see a close connection between the me of my childhood and the me of today. Since I have memories, I infer that it was 'me' who underwent those experiences. I have also inherited certain habitual feelings and views as a result. But the 'me' of my childhood seems at best a distant relation, most definitely not the same person. In fact, to say they are the same person would explicitly contradict the *anātman* doctrine, though to say they are different would also do so. Clearly there is continuity.

This ambiguity about the nature of identity strikes at the heart of the difficulty with any discussion on rebirth, personal continuity, and self-identity. While it is well known that Buddhism denies the idea of an unchanging soul, this is not necessarily the same thing as saying there is no self. This point is well illustrated in a dialogue that takes place between the Buddha and Vacchagotta, a fellow wanderer.[98] Vacchagotta approaches the Buddha with a question about the nature of the self. 'Is there a self?' he demands, but the Buddha remains silent. 'Well, is there not a self?' Again the Buddha remains silent. Receiving no answer, Vacchagotta gets up and leaves, no doubt disappointed and frustrated.

Shortly afterwards, Ānanda, a close disciple of the Buddha, approaches the Buddha and asks him why he failed to answer Vacchagotta's query. The Buddha replies that if he had said there was a self, his reply would not have accorded with the insight that all things are not-self. However, if he had said there was no self, Vacchagotta would have become confused since, where formerly he had a self, he would now no longer have one. This dialogue illustrates the complexity of talking about the nature of the self; it is neither true that there is a self nor is it true to deny it. The implication must be that the reality is something that cannot be fully conceptualized.

This theme is amplified in another dialogue. The Buddha is collecting alms for his daily meal when he is confronted by Kassapa, a naked ascetic, who seems to be desperately concerned about the nature of suffering.[99] 'Is suffering caused by oneself?' he demands. 'No,' replies the Buddha. 'Well, is it created by another?' 'No,' the Buddha again answers. 'Well, is it both created by oneself and another?' demands Kassapa, starting to get a bit exasperated. Once again the Buddha says it is not. Kassapa then asks, 'So has suffering arisen fortuitously then?' 'No,' says the Buddha. 'How is it, then? Is there no suffering?'

speculates Kassapa now completely confused. 'No,' replies the Buddha, 'there is certainly suffering, but that suffering arises in dependence upon conditions. To say that the person who experiences is the same as the one who acts is to fall into eternalism, but to say that the one who acts is different from the one who experiences is to fall into annihilationism.' The Buddha's position is to avoid these two extreme views and follow what he called the Middle Way, which is conceptually expressed through the notion of conditionality.

One of the difficulties inherent in talking about rebirth is that we can easily assume a subtle notion of a permanent self that persists through rebirths and is 'us'. But Buddhism says it is not like that; technically speaking, there is a *conditioned* relationship between one life and the next: on the basis of one being dying, another is born. The relationship is not one of absolute identity, nor of absolute difference, but of conditioned arising.

But it is difficult to break out of the 'I will carry on after death' mind set. In fact, while we are possessed by the delusion of self it is probably impossible. It is impossible for us to conceive of not existing since even when we try to we are still here; it is like trying to see what the grass looks like when we are not looking at it. So even if the rebirth doctrine embodies a meaningful truth, we can but misunderstand and misrepresent that truth, given not only our deluded nature but also the structure of our mind. But some models are more misleading than others, and one that could offer a progressive understanding of rebirth is that of biological reproduction. In the reproductive process, parents pass genes to their offspring, which then shape its growth. Genes comprise information that instructs the proto-embryo to develop into a particular kind of being. If the offspring is human, the genes will lead to the development not only of a human form but a certain eye colour, hair colour, bone structure, etc. While the genes determine all this, the environment will also play a significant role in how the offspring develops. For instance, if it is poorly fed it will not grow properly.

We can apply this model to Karma and rebirth. Rather than thinking of ourselves as undergoing rebirth again and again, we could think of ourselves as the inheritors of a particular genetic disposition, but in this case karmic rather than physical (though there might not be such a clear distinction between them). So our karmic 'genes' shape us: we have tendencies to behave in a certain way, with a certain character and outward personality. Our karmic inheritance is analogous to our physical body: we cannot choose our height or our skin colour (at least not yet). In the same way, we do not choose our character or personality. But just as through regular exercise and healthy living we maximize the welfare of our body, we can, through committed spiritual practice, enable our character to shine forth unencumbered by negative traits. Depending on the quality of our stewardship, the karmic legacy we leave behind may be considerably better or worse for our descendants. We can make emotional deposits in the karmic bank account or we can make withdrawals.

But this notion of a linear descent from being to being, like a business passed down through a family – sometimes expanding, sometimes failing – is only one approach to what rebirth could mean. As long as we hold to the idea of a coherent self, even one that is constantly changing, we will tend to think in terms of a linear descent – one life giving rise to another.

But perhaps it isn't like that at all. Perhaps rebirth isn't individual and linear. Here we begin to question quite fundamentally our notion of constituting a distinctive psychophysical being which, through the rebirth process, gives rise to something closely resembling itself.

Physics has shown that we are not completely separate from our environment – we are in fact part of it – and this is also the Buddhist view. Without active effort, our bodies will simply

degenerate. The world is not a jigsaw made up of discrete interlocking parts, but an indivisible whole, a gestalt, which we
divide into various bits and pieces for the practical purposes of
living. In reality there are no bits and pieces, just an indivisible
totality in which we participate; there is no absolute distinction
between what we are and the world in general. We could say
that we are concentrated nodes of energy. We can understand
this better with the help of an image. Think of custard powder
mixed with milk. If you are like me, when you make custard you
end up with lumps in it. The lumps represent individualized beings and the liquid represents consciousness in general. The
lumps have a degree of cohesion and are distinguishable from
the liquid, but they are still part of it and, if we have a whisk, it is
possible to break them down so that they become indistinguish-
able from the rest of the mixture. Perhaps we are like this, having
no absolute distinctness from other beings or from the world, so
it may be possible for us to resolve back into the cosmic custard.

In reality, there are no hard edges. The experience of life is
more like a spectrum. Where does one colour end and another
begin? So, given that we are not absolutely discrete beings,
could it not be possible to merge with other beings, or even
break up to form several beings, as in the example of the Tibetan
tulku? Could we be the karmic inheritors of several beings
rather than just one, in the same way that a child shares the
genetic inheritance of two parents? We learned earlier that we
impinge on each other all the time – our karmas have implications for other people. We tend to think that when others act in
relation to us we are *essentially* unchanged by that contact –
there is a core that remains. But perhaps it is not like this, perhaps – and this is quite a scary thought – through our contact
with others they become, to some extent, *embodied* within us. So,
to a significant degree, I am perhaps the sum total of all the
people I have ever met and their influence on me. Clearly the

influence (the 'embodiment') that most people exert on us is quite subtle, but we usually have one or two relationships in our lives that have a dramatic impact on who we are and how we develop. We may learn to think like our friend, teacher, or parent. We may even develop the same tastes, habits, or interests, even internalize their voice so that we find them speaking to us and advising us what to do, even directing our decisions. There is a sense in which we even *become* the people we are close to.

In what sense, then, are we separate? In what sense are we 'us'? It would be wrong to conclude from what has been said so far that we must inevitably become clones of those who we are close to, like soft clay bearing the impression of whatever happens to be stamped in it. The extent to which others affect our evolution will depend in part on how determined they are to influence us and in part on how much we resist them, and it is not just one way traffic: through communication, through social interaction, we modify each other just as pebbles in a tumbler rub the rough edges off each other.

It may be that our delusion of a stable identity that lives through all our experience arises from insecurity. While it would be comforting to have a robust identity that withstood the influences of the world, we don't. Whether subtly or grossly, the minds, thoughts, and desires of others find embodiment in us. This can be a source of great anxiety; it can seem as though the 'solidity' of others is constantly threatening to overwhelm our fragile sense of identity. Our mind changes from moment to moment, it seems so quixotic, so insubstantial, we can feel so thin, and we look at others who seem to be so distinctive, continuous, and thick (though inside they feel just as thin as we do). Little wonder, then, that we take refuge in a view that deep down there is something stable and unchanging that defines who we are. But the fact that other minds are an important conditioning factor on who and what we think ourselves to be is not something we need fear. It is because other people can become 'embodied' in us that we can emulate their noble emotions, attitudes, and activities. It is because we can learn to 'channel' the Buddha that we can spiritually awaken. If other people were unable to help reshape our minds we would be rather stuck.

This notion of the minds of other people becoming re-embodied through us is hinted at in the biologist Richard Dawkins' idea of 'memes'.[100] A meme is a unit of cultural transmission; it may be an idea, a piece of music, or a poem. Dawkins uses the concept of memes to explain how culture is transmitted and suggests it can be seen as a new form of evolution.

> Memes propagate themselves in the meme pool by leaping
> from brain to brain via ... imitation.... When you plant a
> fertile meme in my mind you literally parasitize my brain.[101]

With our ideas, thoughts, and emotions we are constantly *colonizing* one another's consciousnesses, and should our own memes take root in another person they can lead to significant transformation. For Dawkins, the key to the survival of any species is its ability to replicate. Memes replicate through imitation, or perhaps emulation would be a better word. But memic influence does not work only through face-to-face experience; memes are embodied in books, in paintings, in sculptures. So through reading the philosopher Heidegger (and notice that we say reading 'him', not just his work), for instance, we can be influenced by that philosopher's memes, we can even begin to enter his mind. If we think of a mind as a series of mental events or spatial plateaus rather than a continuous organic entity, we can – at least for a few illuminated moments – 'become' Heidegger. One of Heidegger's leading ideas was the notion of the 'clearing' (as in a forest) and it may be that through reading and reflecting on Heidegger's ideas we might enter the clearing that was (is?) Heidegger's mind. This can also happen through other cultural media. When I visited the Van Gogh Museum in Amsterdam I felt that, through his canvases, I was being given privileged access to the mind of the artist. I found this mind at once beautiful and frightening since there was no denying that there was something slightly crazed about Van Gogh's perception, intensely alive though it was. In this way, even from beyond the grave, an artist can exert a transformative influence on us, he can begin to colonize us. This is surely a very potent way in which at least some exceptional beings find re-embodiment. It is possible to have an experience of communication with a mind that superficially 'died' even centuries ago. Surely there is something wonderful about this.

So rebirth could be understood as a metaphor that communicates how our conduct can have implications far into the future, perhaps way beyond what we might have imagined. In this respect I am struck by the example of the explorer Ernest Shackleton. In his lifetime, Shackleton was, in many ways, a failure. Not only did he lose out in the race to the South Pole, but he had to abandon several of his expeditions. Yet many people now regard this failed explorer as an example of heroic courage and leadership. Shackleton's overriding principle was safeguarding the welfare of his men, and he went to considerable lengths to save them, including rowing hundreds of miles across the Scotia Sea. Shackleton represents the triumph of the human spirit and comradeship in the face of extreme adversity. For this reason, Shackleton's memory seems to be growing brighter and brighter with time (and even as I write about him now). Whenever someone reads about Shackleton and is inspired to some courageous and heroic act of endurance, Shackleton breathes again through their conduct – his spirit is revived. Paradoxically, Shackleton has probably had a much greater influence on others since his death than he ever did while he was alive.

In this sense, rebirth can be used as a 'thought experiment': we imagine the implications of our actions into the future having a kind of domino effect on the world, even beyond our death. What kind of legacy do we want to leave this world? What kind of example are we offering to other beings? Making this kind of imaginative journey into the future may enable us to gain a better perspective on any action we are proposing to undertake, or even on our life as a whole. While few of us will be as influential as Shackleton or Heidegger, all of us will, nevertheless, exert a significant influence on at least some people; our lives will resound through theirs like the reverberations of a bell. They will then pass that influence on to others. The more we consider this, the more we become aware of the gravity of the present moment – how our conduct irrevocably contributes to the creation of the future, for better or worse, and the more we realize the tremendous responsibility we have by virtue of participating in the world. And there is no way out of this, since even if we were to commit suicide this itself would have implications for others.

The Button Moulder

Not only do we represent the confluence of several karmic streams, or parts of streams, but at death it is possible that we will just flow out into a great karmic ocean, our identity lost for ever. Clearly this possibility of 'losing ourselves' is very frightening. None of us likes to feel we will just get mixed in with everyone else, but why shouldn't it be so? After all, this is what happens to our bodies: they are reabsorbed into the elements. Why should our minds carry on in a discrete form? Ibsen's *Peer Gynt* concludes with a sinister myth that entertains this possibility. Peer, who has never really done anything significant in his life, encounters a character called the button moulder who insists that Peer's destiny is to be taken back into the 'great ladle' and melted down, because his life has been of no consequence. His soul will be melted down and used as raw material for the creation of new souls. As the button moulder says to Peer:

> *You* were designed as a shining button on the coat of the
> world ... but your loop was missing, which is why you must
> go in the pile with the throw-outs to be what is known as
> 'reduced to an ingot'.[102]

Since Peer has lived such a mediocre life, neither especially good nor evil, he is to be melted down. He is not even worth sending to hell. I find this myth psychologically convincing, though quite frightening. If we make nothing of our lives, if we don't develop any particular qualities, any distinctive individuality, any definite direction, what is there to be carried over? So perhaps this is a lesson for us. Because we have found this precious opportunity – as the Vajrayāna would say – we should use it now because who knows whether it will ever come again? We have been given the miraculous vehicle of an individualized consciousness that can make choices, shape its future, and contribute to the welfare or ill of humanity. In the words of a traditional Buddhist image, we have been given a priceless jewel; are we going to cherish it or just throw it away?

We should certainly be wary of falling back on the Buddhist teaching of rebirth as a psychological crutch to alleviate our fear of self-dissolution. The idea that they might one day not exist is an idea that terrifies many people, and it is fruitful to reflect on why this is so. One possible explanation is that deep down they feel their lives are trivial, they have done nothing of any real value. To use an analogy from the Bible, they have buried their talents in the ground rather than adding to them by effort and enterprise.[103] Perhaps there is nothing more tragic than living one's whole life without waking up to its significance.

12

DOES REBIRTH MATTER?

Karma and rebirth were part of the cultural baggage of the ancient Indian Buddhist. For many contemporary Westerners – and even some Easterners – these ideas will not sit comfortably with their understanding of how the universe works, at least in their traditional guises.

Early Buddhism tended to speak of Karma and rebirth in two voices. First, it offered a fairly crude, simplistic model that was able both to account for suffering and to spur people into living a good life through fear of a nasty rebirth and the promise of a pleasant one. It offered a rather neat, even symmetrical, vision of life in which good was always rewarded, and evil was always punished. But like the traditional Christian vocabulary of heaven and hell, this was rather a blunt instrument. As we have seen, this model owes a great deal to pre-existing ideas and its limitations betray these origins.

Secondly, Buddhism talked about Karma in a subtler, more psychological way. This understanding embodies a genuine spiritual advance on what had gone before. With every choice we make, whether overtly expressed or not, we modify our character. Through skilful choices we develop creative habits, whereas through unskilful choices we not only starve our positive impulses but also encourage destructive ones. For better or worse, we are constantly renewing ourselves, even with every passing thought.

But more than this, in modifying our character we also modify our way of relating to the world, which means our experience of the world changes. In an important sense, our world is a creation of our mind. Part of this is the way we influence how others respond to us. But we have seen that this second voice speaks less dogmatically than the first; it allows for many variations, exceptions, and even anomalies. This might be unsatisfactory for some people, but perhaps this reflects the true complexity of experience.

It is fairly easy to accept the doctrine of Karma, at least as expressed in the second voice. We can see how people change because of what they do and the decisions they make. We can also see how this informs their outlook on the world and how others respond to them. But the same is not true of rebirth. We have to stretch our imagination a lot further if we are to take this on. Not only is it not immediately verifiable but it also raises a number of questions that traditional Buddhism has not decisively answered.

Do We Need Rebirth?

Given the cultural origins of the Buddhist teaching of rebirth, is it relevant to the modern world? Had it emerged from a different cultural background, would Buddhism have taught rebirth at all? Such questions invite us to re-examine the status of Buddhist teachings. Do they aim to provide accurate descriptions of reality or are they simply pragmatic? The Buddha's declared aim was to lead people to spiritual liberation, freedom from all limiting beliefs and habits, the transcendence of suffering. He aimed to help others to reproduce in themselves the spiritual awakening that he himself enjoyed, not to indoctrinate them with a system of ideas. Possibly the Buddha talked in terms of rebirth because that is how people then conceived of themselves and their future; he needed to communicate his message in a way they could understand.

Because rebirth was taken to be self-evident, traditional Buddhism did little to argue in its favour. But we live within a very different cultural paradigm, one which does not generally accept rebirth. This means that either the case for rebirth needs to be convincing or the whole area should be left open. But is a belief in rebirth necessary in order to practise Buddhism effectively? While some traditional Buddhists would respond with an emphatic 'yes', it seems to me that the answer is 'no'. Looking at the notion of rebirth pragmatically will help to clarify this.

Buddhism is a practical religion; progress does not consist in a happy consent to holy dogmas but in spiritual evolution, which means transcending selfishness, hatred, and unawareness. Beliefs are relevant in so far as they encourage this process; if they don't, it is not that they are necessarily untrue, just beside the point. So how does a belief in rebirth help us to evolve? Historically, fear of rebirth has functioned not only as a spur to spiritual practice but also as a means of social control; people really believed they would be reborn, and that if they acted badly they would suffer. Buddhist tradition describes in great detail the appalling conditions that will be one's lot if one lives an immoral life. Thus rebirth functioned as a kind of stick that goaded people to change their lives. More subtly, rebirth vividly expresses how our actions have implications beyond ourselves, even beyond our own deaths. Our conduct *does* matter, it *will* influence the future whether we are there to see it or not. Rebirth therefore enables us to recognize the importance of our actions. We cannot contract out of life; whether for better or for worse we *are* going to make a difference.

Despite the Buddha's radical insight that a karma is a volition (*cetanā*) and that one may reap the consequences of one's actions within one's current lifetime, the tendency of early Buddhist scriptures is to understand karmic consequences in terms of what will happen after death. So if one lives a skilful life one will be reborn in a happy realm, if one lives an unskilful life one will be reborn in a realm of suffering. It is clear that the early Buddhists believed that, without fear of retribution after death, people would have no positive motives for acting skilfully, because they would not see the danger in unwholesome motivations.[104] The doctrine of nihilism (*natthikavāda*), as criticized in the Buddhist scriptures, not only denies rebirth but also rejects Karma altogether. It would seem that acceptance of an afterlife was integral to the early Buddhist conception of how Karma worked. The two were seen as inseparable, but they need not be.

If we don't believe in punishment or reward after death, can we really have no motivation to live skilfully? The main issue seems to be finding another means by which to spur us to amend our lives. If we are able to develop a strong volition to live skilfully and strive for spiritual insight, then rebirth may be irrelevant. But in the absence of the 'fear factor' of punishment after death we will need to find another emotional fuel to propel us forward. We will need to see how spiritual practice will lead us to break free from suffering within this life and lead us to a happier, more fulfilled existence. We also need to understand how not taking care of our spiritual life will lead to painful consequences. This requires a more subtle and positive basis for spiritual practice than fear of punishment.

Such a foundation is embodied in the Pali term *saṃvega*, a word that is quite difficult to translate but which indicates an experience that includes, firstly, a realization that life as normally lived is futile and meaningless, and secondly, that we have been foolish and complacent in having let ourselves live so blindly.

Finally, it suggests a vivid sense of urgency to find a way out of the meaningless cycle of mundane life.[105] This final dimension of the experience of *samvega* is particularly crucial because it is the fuel that propels us to search for a way forward. The fact that there is a way out of our predicament, and that we can respond creatively to it, is what leads us towards the experience of spiritual commitment and saves us from existential despair.

It may be that it is only on the basis of a deep experience of *samvega* that spiritual life becomes a possibility. Until we recognize that our lives are lacking, a spiritual path is unnecessary; until we realize we are imprisoned, we are unlikely to want to escape. The philosopher Ludwig Wittgenstein expressed this very well:

> It would be as though someone were first to let me see the hopelessness of my situation and then show me the means of rescue until, of my own accord, or not at any rate led to it by my *instructor*, I ran to it and grasped it.[106]

Some people have said to me that if rebirth wasn't true, and it wasn't possible that we could be reborn in hell or as an animal, they would have no motivation to act ethically and spiritually develop themselves. I find this attitude difficult to understand because, for my own part, the suffering I experience in this very life, the sense of futility and emptiness that sometimes washes through me, are quite enough to motivate me to take care of my existence. At a time when institutions for social regulation were much less developed than they are now, 'cosmic threats' of hell may have been essential in order to keep human beings on the straight and narrow (though they weren't universally successful). But do we still need the fear of hell to spur us to amend our ways? We can enter hell now, in this very lifetime. If we consider for a moment what some human beings have had to endure – the Holocaust, for example – could there be anything much

worse? Heaven and hell are accessible to us right now; we don't
need to think of them as places we might go to after death.

As long as we can motivate ourselves to develop skilful mental
states and eradicate unskilful ones, we can embark on the path
of spiritual transformation. Beliefs about rebirth may be beside
the point. And this is surely one of the most wonderful things
about Buddhism: there is no need to accept a whole range of
unverifiable dogmas before we can practise spiritually. This is a
crucial point, because there is a danger of evaluating how 'good'
a Buddhist one is in terms of how closely one's beliefs accord
with traditional doctrines. However, we don't become better
Buddhists through the uncritical acceptance of traditional
Buddhist dogmas, but by developing wisdom and compassion.

A specious argument sometimes used to defend rebirth is that
to reject it would undermine the principle of dependent origination. We have a certain 'conscious momentum'; surely that
momentum can't just disappear? How can nothing come from
something? This is quite a feeble line of reasoning because it
assumes that our consciousness is independent of our physical
body and can survive without it. But this is the very question at
issue. The principle of dependent origination states that all things
arise in dependence upon conditions, and when those conditions
cease the thing itself ceases. If individualized consciousness is
dependent on the body for its survival, it will disintegrate when
the body dies. No one would insist that it contradicts conditionality to say that a rainbow disappears when the rain stops. We do
not need to think that the rainbow 'carries on' in some way.

What if Rebirth is False?

Are there significant implications for Buddhism as a whole if rebirth is no more than an ancient Indian superstition? What I
have said so far might suggest not, but I think there are. First, if

rebirth does not take place then the content and scope of the Buddhist goal must be re-presented. For instance, one of the most common ways of describing the Buddha's spiritual insight in the early scriptures is known as the three knowledges (*tevijja*).[107] According to this formula, three things were integral to the Buddha's realization: the ability to recollect his manifold past lives, the ability, with his Divine Eye, to see the passing away and reappearance of beings and an understanding of how beings pass on according to their actions, and, finally, the seeing with direct knowledge (*abhiññā*) that he has destroyed all negative inner drives.[108]

So it would seem that, at least for the early Buddhist tradition, an understanding of rebirth was a critical dimension of the awakening experience. What is puzzling about the formula of the three knowledges is that the first two are not the sole preserve of spiritually awakened beings but are, rather, said to be supernormal powers that can be gained through meditative concentration. In other words, it is only the third knowledge – destruction of negative inner drives – that is uniquely characteristic of the Buddhist goal. This makes me wonder why the other two are so emphasized. It is clear that the formulation of a threefold knowledge is an ironic reference to the Brahmanical ideal, which itself focused on three knowledges. These were the Vedas, the orally-transmitted sacred texts. In emphasizing a personal spiritual insight above textual authority, the Buddhist tradition reconceived the meaning of knowledge: it was something the individual realized, not something learned by heart from the elders. This may explain why the first two of the Buddhist three knowledges appear so prominently in early texts: the formula became shorthand for a spiritual experience that to many may already have seemed rather remote. Given that only the destruction of all negative inner drives is a knowledge unique to spiritual awakening, it would seem likely that this particular property discloses the fundamental nature of that experience more than the other two.

Another possibility is that the three knowledges, though seemingly presented as literal realizations, could be understood more metaphorically. On such a reading, the first knowledge could indicate how the Buddha achieved deep insight into his own character. He sees how his past conduct has formed the person he is now, so his habit patterns have become completely transparent to him. The second knowledge shows how the Buddha understood the way in which others condition themselves and their futures. It enables him to read the characters of others, to understand not only where they come from but also where they are heading. The third knowledge illustrates the Buddha's self mastery: he is in control of himself because he is fully conscious, not driven by unconscious desires or habits.

If we discard rebirth as conventionally understood, the traditional Buddhist way of describing our human predicament and the nature of the spiritual enterprise must be re-envisaged. No longer are we aiming to break free from the wheel of birth and death but rather to shake off our spiritual fetters in this very life. This is not an alarming adjustment, but many traditional texts talk about the Buddhist goal in cosmic terms, something to be worked towards over many thousands of lifetimes. If we have just one life, we will have to get a move on: we don't have much time. This could have very positive consequences by generating a sense of urgency and an appreciation of the preciousness of the present moment. If we have thousands of lifetimes before us, we might be tempted into complacency and so slacken our spiritual efforts. By withdrawing attention from the possibility of future lives we can concentrate our attention more keenly on the present. The Buddhist saint becomes a human exemplar, not a cosmic superman: we really *can* emulate him or her, rather than just stand back in awe.

But a rejection of rebirth also calls into question the range of the Buddha's spiritual insight. While some scholars have argued that the Buddha didn't really teach rebirth at all, this charge could be made against all the teachings of early Buddhism: no one knows for certain what the Buddha actually taught. It is at least reasonable to assume that the Buddha not only taught rebirth but was convinced that such a belief was useful in the process of spiritual transformation. If the Buddha thought it was useful, who are we to argue?

I have already drawn attention to the provisional and instrumental nature of beliefs within Buddhism. A 'wrong view' (*micchādiṭṭhi*), according to Buddhism, is not a factually inaccurate one (such as a belief that the moon is made of green cheese) but a perspective that prevents us making spiritual progress. The form and style of the cultural universe in which the Buddha taught inevitably influenced how he communicated his insights. So, for instance, the Buddha made use of traditional Indian cosmology, a cosmology that appears quaintly primitive to today's scientist. Few Buddhists would demand we adopt the ancient Indian view of the universe in its entirety. Rather, we must seek to understand the spiritual message it was used to express. Some of the ways that the Buddha thought and communicated about the world might seem from a modern point of view to be just plain wrong, but this would be to misunderstand their status. We must remember that the Buddha's teachings were a raft, and their measure, therefore, is in how successfully they fulfilled their function. Crucially, the views that foster spiritual transformation need re-evaluation in the light of changing cultural and personal circumstances. This means that had he been around today the Buddha would probably have used different – perhaps even radically different – images and concepts to communicate his message.

Any practitioner of Buddhism must be wary of dogmatic acceptance or rejection of rebirth, and an examination of the motives for taking any particular view will be very instructive. We are often attracted or repelled by certain teachings for psychological reasons. For instance, we might want to live for ever, so we find rebirth comforting, or we might hate ourselves and find the notion of oblivion after death seductive. At the same time, we shouldn't feel obliged to conform with a dogma simply because it has been a historical part of the spiritual tradition we have adopted, neither should we pretend to be convinced by a doctrine we think is culturally redundant. Following a spiritual path is not about subscribing to rigid dogmas but about overcoming selfishness and hatred and seeing our lives with complete clarity.

A pragmatic approach to Karma and rebirth I have found quite reassuring is the one found in the *Kālāmu Suttu*.[109] In this text, the Buddha points out that a man who lives a committed ethical life can be assured of four things: (1) if Karma and rebirth are true, then, owing to his skilful life he will be reborn after death in a good destination, even in a heaven world, (2) if rebirth is not true he will have lived a joyful life anyway, happy and free from ill will, (3) if evil conduct reaps suffering, the ethical person has nothing to fear because he has not acted evilly, (4) if evil conduct does not lead to painful consequences, then the ethical person has nothing to fear anyway.

The most important thing, then, is to live a skilful, compassionate life. If we do this, we need not worry about what may or may not happen after death, since if there is rebirth we will have established a wholesome foundation for our next existence, and if there is no rebirth it won't concern us. We need not rely on the possibility of some 'reward' after death because there are great benefits to be gained here and now through spiritual practice.

13

CONCLUSION: THE INTERCONNECTED SELF

The traditional Buddhist teachings of Karma and rebirth express how our actions of body, speech, and mind have implications not only for ourselves but also for others, and even the world in general. Moment by moment we create and recreate ourselves through what we think, say, and do. Over time, we develop distinctive habits: a recognizable 'self' that makes us more likely to perpetuate those habits rather than adopt others. We get stuck in a rut. This is how most of us experience our lives most of the time: trapped in patterns of thought and behaviour that we can neither break out of nor see beyond. Our habits become the limit of our world and our range of choices becomes very narrow. Like blinkered cart-horses ploughing the same old furrow, we cut deeper and deeper gashes into the earth of life.

But our lives are also intimately connected to others. We are not detached selves isolated from everything and everyone but interconnected selves whose actions influence, and are influenced by, those around us. To be human is to relate to other human beings. Not only do our actions have implications for others in the present but they can also affect people who have not yet been born. Recognizing this helps us to understand that how we conduct our lives is a serious matter. Our conduct can add to the sum total of goodness in the world or it can eat away at that goodness by adding to what is base. It may often seem as though our lives have no lasting value, and this can encourage us to cling to some consolatory hope of a life yet to come, but it is difficult to see our own life in perspective, difficult to recognize exactly the impact we have had – for better or worse. It is difficult to see what our life might have been like if we hadn't performed good deeds (or bad). It might be a useful thought experiment to imagine what life would have been like had we never been born: would the world be a better or a worse place?

This device underlies the film *It's a Wonderful Life*.[110] The film tells the story of George Bailey. In many ways, George is very ordinary; he lives in the same small town all his life (though he has aspirations to travel and do something 'big'), works in a finance company, has a wife and children. In many ways his life is quite humdrum. Towards the end of the film, owing to his uncle misplacing a large sum of money, George stands to lose his whole business and might even end up in jail. He becomes so desperate that he wishes he had never been born and decides to kill himself; a somewhat sad end to an unremarkable life, perhaps.

But George's life is really rather remarkable. He cherishes personal ambitions but situations arise that seem to demand that he renounce his own desires in order to respond to the needs of those around him. His whole life is a continual struggle between personal desire and objective need, and he always chooses to respond to the need. But where has this got him? George thinks it has got him nowhere and he becomes a poor, wretched man on the brink of ruin and suicide.

Just as George is about to throw himself from a bridge, an angel arrives and throws himself into the icy water. George dives into the river to save him. Later, unconsoled, George still wishes he had never been born. The angel grants his wish by showing him how life in the town would have progressed without him. For example, George's brother is dead (since George would not have saved him from drowning as a child), so he never grew up to be a war hero who saved many people's lives. The town as a whole is dramatically different. It is characterized by harsh, selfish behaviour and is in the grip of a heartless property tycoon who keeps many of the residents in poverty by charging exorbitant rents.

George begins to realize that, while thwarting his personal ambition, the many sacrifices he made throughout his life have benefited the town immeasurably, adding to the quantum of decency, kindness, and solidarity of its citizens. While caught up in the whirl of daily life, George is unable to recognize his positive impact on the lives of others. Through stepping back and contemplating a world in which none of his little acts of kindness had happened he sees the true value of his contribution. He sees how seemingly small kindnesses snowball into the future to set up dramatically positive chains of events. He appreciates how rich he has become as an individual through his compassionate action and is finally able to lay to rest his regret at his unfulfilled ambitions.

It is easy to underestimate the impact of everyday kindnesses and cruelties. It is often only with time that the true character and influence of such actions can be seen. While the traditional Buddhist doctrines of Karma and rebirth may present themselves in a somewhat archaic, even naive, guise, they nevertheless communicate timeless truths about what it means to be human. We bear a responsibility to our future self and to other human beings through what we do. We have the power to transform the world for good or ill. It is through the compassionate exercise of this power that we fulfil our responsibility to life and transcend the confines of our ordinary mind. We place a feather on the scales of life that tips them towards goodness.

NOTES AND REFERENCES

1   Sangharakshita (trans.), *Dhammapada*, Windhorse Publications, 2001, verses 1–2, p.13

2   *Alagaddūpama Sutta* (*Majjhima Nikāya* 22)

3   This can be seen in, for example, the *Tevijja Sutta* (*Dīgha Nikāya* 13), and is explored in Michael Pye, *Skilful Means*, Duckworth, 1978, pp.126–30

4   Ganganatha Jha (trans.), *Śāntarakṣita's Tattvasaṅgraha*, Motilal Banarsidass, Delhi 1939, verse 3344.

5   Paul Tillich, *Dynamics of Faith*, Harper Torchbooks, New York, 1958, pp.49–51

6   Luke 24:13

7   Richard Holloway, *Doubts and Loves: What is Left of Christianity*, Canongate Books, 2001, p.59

8   Martin Heidegger, *Basic Writings*, Routledge, 1993, p.431

9   Directed by Christopher Nolan, 2000

10 *Cūḷakammavibhaṅga Sutta* (*Majjhima Nikāya* 135)

11 Bhikkhu Ñāṇamoli and Bhikkhu Bodhi (trans.), *The Middle Length Discourses of the Buddha*, Wisdom Publications, 1995, p.1053

12 Christmas Humphreys, *Karma and Rebirth*, Curzon Press, 1994

13 This understanding of Karma seems to be derived from the Theosophy of H.P. Blavatsky.

14   See Steven Collins, *Selfless Persons*, Cambridge, 1982, chapter 1

15   Ibid. p.46

16   Ibid. p.54

17   Ibid. p.52

18   *Kukkuravatika Sutta* (*Majjhima Nikāya* 57)

19   Richard F. Gombrich, *How Buddhism Began: the Conditioned Genesis of the Early Buddhist Teachings*, Athlone, London 1996

20   *Majjhima Nikāya* 56

21   Some of the ancient Hindu texts called the Purāṇas put forward this view.

22   *Tittha Sutta* (*Aṅguttara Nikāya* 3.61)

23   *Cūḷakammavibhaṅgha Sutta* (*Majjhima Nikāya* 135)

24   *Majjhima Nikāya* 101

25   See also the *Tittha Sutta* (*Aṅguttara Nikāya* 3.61)

26   *Dhammapada*, op. cit., verse 165

27   In the *Avataṃsaka* or 'Flower Ornament' *Sūtra*

28   Richard Hayes, *Land of No Buddha*, Windhorse Publications, Birmingham 1998, p.76

29   Their story is told in Thomas Keneally's book, *Schindler's Ark*, Hodder, 1982

30   Sogyal Rimpoche, *The Tibetan Book of Living and Dying*, Rider, London 1992, p.96

31   Ani Pachen and Adelaide Donnelley, *Sorrow Mountain*, Doubleday, 2000

32   Ibid. p.143

33   *The Times*, 26 June 2002, p.15

34   *The Times*, 1 November 2002, pp.1 & 5

35   *Moḷiyasīvaka Sutta* (*Saṃyutta Nikāya* 36.21)

36   The same list of causal factors is found in the *Putta Sutta* (*Aṅguttara Nikāya* 4.87), the *Ṭāna Sutta* (*Aṅguttara Nikāya* 4.125), and the *Girimānanda Sutta* (*Aṅguttara Nikāya* 10.60).

37   Trans. T.W. Rhys Davids 1894, and still in print.

38   Bhikkhu Pesala (ed.), *The Debate of King Milinda*, Motilal Banarsidass, Delhi 1991, p.39

39   Buddhaghosa, *Aṭṭhasālini*, Pe Maung Tin (trans.), Pali Text Society, 1976, ii.360

40   For expositions of the *dharma-niyama* see Sangharakshita, *Who is the Buddha?* Windhorse Publications, Birmingham 1995, pp.105–8

41   *Luke* 6: 27–8

42   For more about Kṣitigarbha, see Vessantara, *Meeting the Buddhas*, Windhorse Publications, Glasgow 1993, pp.198–201

43   *Aññatitthiya Sutta* (*Saṃyutta Nikāya* 12.24). The three following suttas make exactly the same point.

44   Sangharakshita, *The Three Jewels*, Windhorse Publications, Birmingham 1998, pp.62–3

45   *Nibbedhika Sutta, Aṅguttara Nikāya* iii.65

46   This point is debated in the *Upāli Sutta* (*Majjhima Nikāya* 56)

47   *Lobha, dveṣa,* and *moha*

48   See, for example, the *Parikuppa Sutta* (*Aṅguttara Nikāya* 5.129)

49   *Rūpa, vedanā, saṃjñā, saṃskāras,* and *vijñāna*

50   *Majjhima Nikāya* 135

51   *Udāna* 5.3

52   *Dhammapada* op. cit., verse 127

53   *Majjhima Nikāya* 136

54   cf. *Dhammapada*, verses 137–40

55   *Dhammapada*, verse 240

56   Brian Keenan, *An Evil Cradling*, Vintage, 1993

57   J.B. Priestley, *An Inspector Calls and Other Plays*, Penguin, 2001

58   Ibid. p.207

59   Ibid. p.219

60   *Aṅguttara Nikāya* 3.99

61   Nicholas Tomalin et al., *The Strange Last Voyage of Donald Crowhurst* International Marine/Ragged Mountain Press, 2001

62   *Saṃyutta Nikāya* 42.6

63   Richard Gombrich, *Buddhist Precept and Practice*, Motilal Banarsidass, Delhi 1991

64   This included the Vaibhāṣikas, the adherents of a later phase of the Sarvāstivada school, see Richard Gombrich, *How Buddhism Began*, op. cit., p.56

65   Ibid. p.57. Canonical references expounding this view include the *Vimāna Vatthu* and the *Nidhikaṇḍa Sutta* (both in the *Khuddhaka Nikāya*).

66   *Acts* 9:1–19

67   Ibid. 9:4

68   *Aṅgulimāla Sutta* (*Majjhima Nikāya* 86)

69   Directed by Peter Weir, 1998

70   *Hamlet* iii.1

71   Edward Conze, a renowned Buddhist scholar, has suggested three reasons why 'rich old women' have been attracted to the rebirth doctrine. First, it allows them to believe that in the past they have lived romantic existences as Egyptian princesses and the like; secondly, it frees them from the sense of social guilt endemic in bourgeois society by persuading them that they deserve their wealth and privileges as a reward for previous merit; and thirdly it convinces them that their precious selves will not be lost when they die. *Memoirs of a Modern Gnostic*, vol.2, Samizdat Publishing Company, Sherborne 1979, p.33.

72   Ninian Smart, *Doctrine and Argument in Indian Philosophy*, Allen and Unwin, 1964, p.159, points out that only the Materialists denied rebirth; after they died out rebirth was no longer an issue.

73   Bhikkhu Pesala, *The Debate of King Milinda*, op. cit., p.10

74   Ibid. p.12

75   See for instance the *Mahātaṇhāsaṅkhaya Sutta* (*Majjhima Nikāya* 38)

76   For example the Vaibhāṣikas, for more information see Richard Gombrich, *How Buddhism Began*, op. cit., p.56

77   For a slightly fuller account of these views see James P. McDermott, 'Karma and Rebirth in Early Buddhism,' in Wendy Doniger

O'Flaherty, *Karma and Rebirth in Classical Indian Traditions*, Motilal Banarsidass, Delhi 1983

78   *Cūḷamālunkya Sutta* (*Majjhima Nikāya* 63)

79   Each of these questions is posed in terms of a 'tetralemma', which takes the following form: (1) Is it A? (2) Is it not A? (3) Is it both A and not A? (4) Is it neither A nor not A?

80   In some accounts the inhabitants of the angry god realm are divided between the preta and the god realms. For more information see *Abhidharmakośabhāṣyam*, Asian Humanities Press, 1991, vol.2, p.500, n.26.

81   *Majjhima Nikāya* 129.24

82   For more on the traditional descriptions of the hells see the *Devadūta Sutta* (*Majjhima Nikāya* 130)

83   From *The Lotos-Eaters* (1835)

84   For a translation see Robert Thurman (trans.), *The Tibetan Book of the Dead*, HarperCollins, 1998

85   This thesis requires a very close and involved reading of the early texts. See Peter Harvey, *The Selfless Mind*, RoutledgeCurzon, 1995, especially chapter 6.

86   There is said to be a type of non-returner (*anāgāmin*) who attains spiritual awakening in the intermediate state. See, for example, the *Saṃyojana Sutta* (*Aṅguttara Nikāya* 4.131). This view would seem to presuppose a belief in an intermediate state.

87   The following account of the intermediate state is taken from Vasubandhu's *Abhidharmakośabhāṣyam*, trans. Leo M. Pruden, Asian Humanities Press, Berkeley 1991, vol.2, chapter 3.

88   The Divine Eye or *dibbacakkhu* is a supernormal power which supposedly enables its possessor to see the passing away and re-appearance of beings in accordance with their karma. See, for instance, the *Mahā-Assapura Sutta* (*Majjhima Nikāya* 39.20)

89   Glenn H. Mullin, *Death and Dying in the Tibetan Tradition*, Arkana, 1986

90   Vicki MacKenzie, *Reborn in the West*, HarperCollins, 1997

91   Ibid.

92   Morey Bernstein, *The Search for Bridey Murphy*, Doubleday, 1989; *The Search for Bridey Murphy*, directed by Noel Langley, 1956

93   e.g. *Twenty Cases Suggestive of Reincarnation*, University Press of Virginia, Charlottesville 1995

94   Tom Shroder, *Old Souls: The Scientific Search for Evidence of Past Lives*, Simon and Schuster, 2001

95   Ibid. p.173

96   Ibid. p.239

97   See David Bishai, 'Can Population Growth Rule out Reincarnation? A Model of Circular Migration', *Journal of Scientific Exploration*, vol.14, no.3, pp.411–420, 2000

98   *Ānanda Sutta* (*Saṃyutta Nikāya* 44.10)

99   *Acela Sutta* (*Saṃyutta Nikāya* 12.17)

100   Richard Dawkins, *The Selfish Gene*, Oxford, 1976

101   Ibid. pp.206–7

102   Henrik Ibsen, *Peer Gynt*, trans. Peter Watts, Penguin, 1970, p.199

103   *Matthew* 25:14ff

104   See, for example, *Apaṇṇaka Sutta* (*Majjhima Nikāya* 60.5–9)

105   'Affirming the Truths of the Heart: The Buddhist Teachings on Saṃvega and Pasada', http://www.accesstoinsight.org/lib/modern/thanissaro/affirming.html

106   Anthony Kenny (ed.), *The Wittgenstein Reader*, Blackwell, 1994, p.302

107   *Mahā-Assapura Sutta* (*Majjhima Nikāya* 39.19–21 and *passim*)

108   *Pubbe nivāsānussati-ñāṇa, dibba-cakkhu-ñāṇa*, and *āsava-kkhaya-ñāṇa* respectively.

109   *Aṅguttara Nikāya* 3.65

110   Directed by Frank Capra, 1947

FURTHER READING

Traditional Sources

There are many references to Karma and rebirth in the early Buddhist scriptures. These are some of the more important.

The Shorter Exposition on Karma (*Cūḷakammavibhaṅga Sutta, Majjhima Nikāya* 135)
A 'classic' explanation of Karma as the primary means of explaining all manner of differences between people, from economic inequality to personal appearance.

The Greater Exposition on Karma (*Mahākammavibhaṅga Sutta, Majjhima Nikāya* 136)
This sutta emphasizes how the workings of Karma are not always obvious on the surface. For instance, someone can act badly and seem to be rewarded, or vice versa. Sooner or later, however, the fruits of their Karma will be realized.

The Discourse with Upāli (*Upāli Sutta, Majjhima Nikāya* 56)
This entertaining sutta, in which the Buddha converts Upāli, a Jain, emphasizes the primacy of mind in Karma.

The Dog-Duty Ascetic (*Kukkuravatika Sutta, Majjhima Nikāya* 57)
This ironic and humorous sutta shows that different intentions bring
about different kinds of results – ethical impulses can be mixed.

The Discourse at Devadaha (*Devadaha Sutta, Majjhima Nikāya* 101)
In this fascinating sutta, the Buddha gets into dialogue with a group of
Jain ascetics and helps them realize that their view of Karma is limited. In
doing so, he presents his own view.

The Salt Crystal (*Lonaphala Sutta, Aṅguttara Nikāya* 3.99)
This sutta shows how the effects of Karma differ according to the ethical
condition of the agent.

Sīvaka with the Top-knot (*Moḷiyasīvaka Sutta, Saṃyutta Nikāya* 36.21)
This little-known but very important sutta encapsulates the view that not
everything that happens is a result of Karma; there are other causal
conditions.

From the Western Country (*Pacchābhūmaka Sutta, Saṃyutta Nikāya* 42.6)
This delightful sutta illustrates how Karma is a natural principle that can't
be circumvented by, for instance, magic.

The Conch (*Saṅkha Sutta, Saṃyutta Nikāya* 42.8)
This sutta criticizes the simplistic view that 'whatever one does frequently
will determine one's future rebirth'. Some evil actions only take a short
time to complete but can have a significant effect.

Translations

Bhikkhu Ñāṇamoli and Bhikkhu Bodhi (trans.), *The Middle Length Discourses
of the Buddha (Majjhima Nikāya)*, Wisdom Publications, Boston 1995

Bhikkhu Bodhi (trans.), *The Connected Discourses of the Buddha (Saṃyutta
Nikāya)*, Wisdom Publications, Boston 2000.

Commentaries

Steven Collins, *Selfless Persons*, Cambridge, 1982
This academic work includes important background discussions on the evolution of the Buddhist doctrines of Karma and rebirth.

Peter Harvey, *The Selfless Mind*, Curzon, 1995
This academic work examines a number of important themes relating to the teachings of Karma and rebirth, such as the nature of the self in Buddhism.

Christmas Humphreys, *Karma and Rebirth*, Curzon, 1994
Originally published in the 1940s, this well written book is somewhat compromised by heavy reliance on Theosophy and a lack of understanding of the *niyamas*. It conflates Karma with the general principle of dependent origination.

Geshe Kelsang Gyatso, *Living Meaningfully, Dying Joyfully*, Tharpa, 1999
A presentation of traditional Tibetan Buddhist views in relation to death and rebirth.

Glenn H. Mullin, *Death and Dying: The Tibetan Tradition*, Arkana, 1986
Contains valuable material relating to the Tibetan tradition.

Richard F. Gombrich, *How Buddhism Began: the Conditioned Genesis of the Early Buddhist Teachings*, Athlone, London 1996
This extremely insightful academic work includes detailed discussion of the origins and development of Buddhist notions of Karma.

Wendy Doniger O'Flaherty, *Karma and Rebirth in Classical Indian Traditions*, Motilal Banarsidass, Delhi 1983
Though seriously academic, this work helps place Buddhist ideas on Karma and rebirth in the broader Indian socio-religious context.

Vicki MacKenzie, *Reborn in the West*, HarperCollins, 1997
This fascinating popular book includes a number of case studies of Buddhists supposedly reborn in the West.

Bhikkhu Pesala, *The Debate of King Milinda*, Motilal Banarsidass, Delhi 1991
An abridged translation of a Pali work which includes detailed discussions
of issues relating to Karma and rebirth, suggesting that these were very
live issues in the early Buddhist tradition.

Sangharakshita, *The Three Jewels*, Windhorse Publications, Birmingham 1998
Places Buddhist notions of Karma and rebirth in the context of the overall
Buddhist view, including Buddhist cosmology.

Sangharakshita, *Who is the Buddha?* Windhorse Publications, Birmingham
1994
Chapter 7 contains a succinct overview of a number of important issues
relating to Karma and rebirth.

Tom Shroder, *Old Souls*, Simon and Schuster, 2001
The very readable record of a journalist's travels with Professor Ian
Stevenson, the notable investigator of past-life claims.

Francis Story, *Rebirth as Doctrine and Experience: Essays and Case Studies*,
Buddhist Publication Society, 1975
This book relies on the work of Ian Stevenson, presenting case studies
intended to support the reality of rebirth.

Subhuti, *The Buddhist Vision*, Windhorse Publications, Birmingham 2001
This book treats many issues of relevance to the themes of Karma and
rebirth from the point of view of a modern Western reader.

Robert A.F. Thurman (trans.), *The Tibetan Book of the Dead*, HarperCollins,
1998
One of several translations of the classic Tibetan account of death, the
intermediate state, and rebirth.

Martin Willson, *Rebirth and the Western Buddhist*, Wisdom Publications,
1987
Not quite what is purports to be, this short book offers an account of the
Tibetan view of Karma and rebirth.

INDEX

The windhorse symbolizes the energy of the Enlightened mind carrying the truth of the Buddha's teachings to all corners of the world. On its back the windhorse bears three jewels: a brilliant gold jewel represents the Buddha, the ideal of Enlightenment, a sparkling blue jewel represents the teachings of the Buddha, the Dharma, and a glowing red jewel, the community of the Buddha's enlightened followers, the Sangha. Windhorse Publications, through the medium of books, similarly takes these three jewels out to the world.

Windhorse Publications is a Buddhist publishing house, staffed by practising Buddhists. We place great emphasis on producing books of high quality, accessible and relevant to those interested in Buddhism at whatever level. Drawing on the whole range of the Buddhist tradition, Windhorse books include translations of traditional texts, commentaries, books that make links with Western culture and ways of life, biographies of Buddhists, and manuals on meditation.

As a charitable institution we welcome donations to help us continue our work. We also welcome manuscripts on aspects of Buddhism or meditation. For orders and catalogues log on to www.windhorsepublications. com or contact

WINDHORSE PUBLICATIONS   WINDHORSE BOOKS   CONSORTIUM
11 PARK ROAD   P O BOX 574   1045 WESTGATE DRIVE
BIRMINGHAM   NEWTOWN NSW 2042   ST PAUL MN 55114
B13 8AB   AUSTRALIA   USA
UK

Windhorse Publications is an arm of the Friends of the Western Buddhist Order, which has more than sixty centres on five continents. Through these centres, members of the Western Buddhist Order offer regular programmes of events for the general public and for more experienced students. These include meditation classes, public talks, study on Buddhist themes and texts, and 'bodywork' classes such as t'ai chi, yoga, and massage. The FWBO also runs several retreat centres and the Karuna Trust, a fund-raising charity that supports social welfare projects in the slums and villages of India.

Many FWBO centres have residential spiritual communities and ethical businesses associated with them. Arts activities are encouraged too, as is the development of strong bonds of friendship between people who share the same ideals. In this way the FWBO is developing a unique approach to Buddhism, not simply as a set of techniques, less still as an exotic cultural interest, but as a creatively directed way of life for people living in the modern world.

If you would like more information about the FWBO visit the website at www.fwbo.org or write to

LONDON BUDDHIST CENTRE   ARYALOKA
51 ROMAN ROAD   HEARTWOOD CIRCLE
LONDON   NEWMARKET
E2 OHU   NH 03857
UK   USA